The God of Tech

Modern technology, its Divine origin, and
activating the next great movement of God
through Spirit-led innovation

RYAN COLLINS

FOREWORD

Have you ever considered the amount of faith it took to advance the most transformative inventions in the world today? Consider sitting with the discovery that light is an electromagnetic wave knowing you would have to convince people that something completely invisible to the human eye was powerful enough to cause light to shine!

Scientific inventions have required immense amounts of faith since the dawn of time, yet the technological field has exceedingly become a humanistic sphere of society, often dedicated to the eradication of God as the Creator and devoted to evolutionary doctrine. I'd propose that believers are needed in the technological space more than ever; not simply for the salvation of souls or to simply shift the mortal dogma that has infiltrated science textbooks and technological conventions, but through a believer's divine advantage, display the brilliance of the Creator.

In the pages you are about to read Ryan Collins powerfully illustrates the history of faith in modern-day innovation and science with great hope that the next move of God will be filled with believers that actualize the divine brilliance inside of them to move humanity toward heavenly solutions.

Several years ago I had the honor of joining Ryan Collins and a team from Bethel School of Technology at a gathering with about two hundred Google employees at Google's headquarters for a session on the topic of: "Furthering the Narrative around Christianity's Impact in the Tech Space." Some of the brightest minds were in attendance, including several Google team members who worked in the artificial intelligence (AI) division.

It was a privilege and an honor to be a part of the thought leadership taking place that day. Yet, I became aware that some of the greatest minds in the modern day have bypassed a deeper dimension of brilliance. The two quotients: I.Q. and E.Q. are commonly known to analyze our minds and emotions, but rarely is spiritual intelligence utilized in the efforts to pioneer new discoveries that serve society.

Yet, as believers, we have access to the scientist of all scientists, doctor of all doctors, and engineer of all engineers through the power of the Holy Spirit. We have the capacity for brilliance that is beyond human reason and transcends the logic of the leading intellectuals. This transcendent advantage grants us the ability to think like God in real-time (1 Corinthians 12:16).

As Ryan says in his book "The very nature of its science will reveal the brilliance of our Creator and His relationship with creation. And, it will be fully actualized by Christ-followers receiving spiritual downloads from God to move humanity heavenward." This is a beautiful explanation of the importance of believers operating as the sanctified solutionaries that we are designed to be. The purpose of these divine explorations is not for personal achievements or accolades, but to tread the path of innovative discoveries with eternal significance. In the depths of these pages, you will be filled with faith for the next genius move of God and grow expectant for how He will partner with you in displaying His glory on the earth.

Kris Vallotton
Best-selling Author
Senior Associate Leader, Bethel Church

CONTENTS

Introduction   1

Chapter One: Redeeming Tech   10

Chapter Two: The Counterfeit   24

Chapter Three: In the Name of Science   48

Chapter Four: Hacking Humans   67

Chapter Five: Where was the Church?   78

Chapter Six: The Next Epoch   86

Chapter Seven: A Moonshot Factory   106

Chapter Eight: Spiritual Intelligence   152

Chapter Nine: Yada Relationship   170

Chapter Ten: One Red Dot   202

About the Author   209

Works Cited   210

INTRODUCTION

A NUN. A HEALING WELL. AND THE FUTURE OF TECHNOLOGY.

In the mid-7th century, during the rapid expansion and Christian conversion of the English kingdom of Mercia, there lived a young woman named Frideswide. Born to a Mercian sub-king and his wife, in what is now modern-day Oxford, Frideswide grew up learning the gospel of Jesus under her tutor, Elgitha.

Elgitha greatly influenced Frideswide, teaching her that "whatever is not God is nothing." Or, stated another way: without God nothing is worth pursuing. This soon became Frideswide's worldview; and as a teenager, she committed to serve Christ in chastity as a nun, eventually becoming the abbess of a local monastery.

Frideswide was well known throughout the kingdom for her beauty and royal inheritance, and she caught the attention of a prince named Aelfgar, who sent a messenger to her, requesting her hand in marriage. The nun rejected the proposal, but Aelfgar would not relent.[1]

Infuriated, he sent an army of men to abduct Frideswide

by force and bring her to his palace to be his bride. However, spies warned her of the prince's plan, and she, along with two of her fellow nuns, fled to the banks of the River Thames. There, they found a young man clothed in white with a boat.

The man in white was an angel sent by God to rescue the nuns. He took them down the river, where they fled by foot through a deep forest and eventually took refuge in an abandoned pigsty, turning it into a place of worship.

And next to the pigsty, there appeared a well.

For three years, Frideswide and the two other nuns sought refuge in the pigsty, drinking from a well that first came into being when Frideswide prayed for fresh water. Frideswide partnered with God to manifest a heavenly solution for an earthly problem, pulling from an unseen reality into the physical world.

It was a phenomenon - a sign and wonder from another realm. It was a miracle from heaven.

All the while, in his maniacal pursuit, Aelfgar devised another plan that was sure to bring him his bride. He and his army of men stormed the city gates of Oxford, demanding to know Frideswide's whereabouts or they would burn the city to the ground. Fearing for their lives, the people of Oxford gave up her location.

Aelfgar sent two messengers to Frideswide with gifts and songs as one last attempt to change her mind. But Frideswide held steadfast, stating that Christ was her only Bridegroom.

An enraged Aelfgar rode into the forest, his cronies falling behind on their horses, to betroth Frideswide by any means necessary. Near their refuge, Frideswide's two companions

heard the prince barreling closer and closer, and they rushed
to warn her of the imminent danger.

But Frideswide would rather have died upholding her
covenant with God than give herself to Aelfgar because
whatever is not God is nothing. And, in a 7th-century Anglo-Saxon
Kingdom such as Mercia, forced compliance to the prince or
death were the only possible options in Frideswide's situation.

Except, God has a habit of working in the realm of the
impossible.

Frideswide prayed and God protected her, striking Aelfgar
blind as he drew within hand's distance of the nun. The
prince fell to the ground and cried out for help. Begging to
see again, he repented for all he had done to her and swore
that he would leave her alone.

Frideswide had compassion on Aelfgar, and led the blind,
begging prince to her miracle well. She cleansed Aelfgar's eyes
in the water, and he could see again. God healed Aelfgar
through the prayer of the very nun he was trying to abduct,
and the well became a place of healing for centuries to come.

II.

Simon Jackman is a Senior Innovation Fellow at Oxford
University. He works with some of the leading tech and space
companies in the world, putting into application the most
advanced and emerging technologies to achieve the
impossible. His meetings range from ending world hunger to
interplanetary habitation.

Simon is also helping to lead a School of the Spirit at

Oxford Community Church. He and his fellow Christ-followers are devoted to ushering in an outpouring of the Holy Spirit across the globe, starting in a geography that was once known for its deep reverence to God and marked by His signs and wonders, like Frideswide's well.*

Simon and I first met shortly after he attended a conference at my home church, Bethel, in Redding, CA. Quickly, we became friends, meeting regularly over video chat to dream together and minister to each other. He introduced me to the story of Saint Frideswide during a conversation we were having about Britain's fertile history of scientific discovery and technological innovation stemming from Divine wisdom and revelation.

I posed the question to Simon, "What if the key to unlocking the next great wave of technological innovation is to rediscover its origins from the perspective of God the Creator partnering with humanity to materialize heavenly solutions for earthly problems?"

Inversely, what if the next great revival is dependent upon fully actualizing technology so that all would taste and see the Lord's goodness? What if science is meant to point to Emmanuel, Christ with us? And, what if it can only go as far as we are willing to discover and unveil the goodness of God with the mind of Christ that has been given to us as His sons and daughters?

Here is what Simon shared:

---

* Oxford University was founded in 1096. Its motto is 'Dominus Illuminatio Mea', which means 'The Lord is my Light'. For its first 500 years, the school taught theology before any other subject because they believed you couldn't know anything without knowing God first.

In the fields at the side of where Frideswide's Abbey stood, over 1,000 years later stands a large building bought by a group of newer churches as a hub for worshiping God, for education and as an apostolic base to send kingdom people around the world. It just happens to be a building where the first ever magnets were produced for imaging people—at its time the greatest breakthrough in diagnosis since X-rays. This building is now at the very heart of a new Innovation Quarter being designed by the University for the city, with investment of several billions of dollars lined up—a location for global technology companies, start-ups and research labs.

Simon then added:

Frideswide prayed to God for water and a well opened up which became a source of healing and pilgrimage for people. It's still there today, but the healing has dried up. It's time to re-dig the wells of God's Spirit in this place and to see new technologies invented and developed.

This is a book about re-digging the wells of Living Water. It's about rediscovering the Divine origins of our modern technologies to unlock the next season of tech innovation, solving earthly problems with heavenly solutions. It's about revealing the truth of our existence - that we were created on purpose and for a purpose - and threshing out the false narrative that we evolved from an accident. But above all else, like the story of Frideswide's well, it's an invitation to partner with the Holy Spirit in the realm of the impossible to catalyze the next great movement of God so that all would taste and see His goodness.

We are at the tipping point of a new epoch* in which the greatest intellect will come from faith in God. In fact, we are currently living in an epoch of scientific innovation that was birthed from man's partnership with the Holy Spirit over a century ago, and the desire for God to give us a spirit of wisdom and revelation by enlightening the eyes of our understanding through knowing Him (Ephesians 1:17-18).

I've often heard it said that innovation moves humanity forward. The question is: "forward to what?" Forward denotes an intended direction. Therefore, in order to know which way is forward, we must first identify our destination.

I love how my wife, Briana, puts it, "Innovation's true intent is to move us heavenward." This is the destination. But, it's not a destination measured within the confines of space and time. It is not a journey from point A to point B. It is a matter of point A and B being inextricably and eternally linked. The destination is found in the presence of God, of which there is no end to His goodness and glory.

We are the temple of God in which His Spirit resides (I Corinthians 3:16), and we are seated in heavenly places in Christ Jesus (Ephesians 2:6). Heaven is in us and we are in heaven. We carry heaven on earth wherever we go and activate its final say in every situation, restored by the work of the cross and resurrection of Christ.

Jesus said to the Pharisee, Nicodemus, in John 3:3 "Unless one is born again, he cannot see the Kingdom of God." The

---

* An epoch is an extended period of time marked by a series of favorable events.

Kingdom of God is not a place alone, but also a person, the Christ, who stood before Nicodemus's very own eyes. And yet, Nicodemus could not see.

"How can this be?" he asked Jesus. To which Jesus replied, "We speak what We know and testify what We have seen, and you do not receive our witness. If I have told you earthly things and you do not believe, how will you believe if I tell you heavenly things?" (John 3:11-12 NKJV)

The world operates in a "see-to-believe" paradigm, but Jesus flipped the script with a "believing is seeing" heaven-on-earth revelation and an invitation to live by faith and not by sight (2 Corinthians 5:7). It is often said that Jesus came to turn the world upside down. In reality, He came to turn the world right side up and restore it to its original design.

The revelation of Jesus is the unveiling of Emmanuel, Christ with us and in us, to the world. He is an invitation to see with our hearts a superior reality rooted in Love Personified, for God is love (1 John 4:8). And, the evidence of this superior reality can be seen in the manifestations of the invisible realm that drive our modern world.

At no other point in recorded history has humanity functioned in an invisible realm more than we do in today's society. Think about it. We video chat with friends thousands of miles away, airdrop pictures from one device to another, and flip through hundreds of television channels receiving radio waves from a satellite hovering in outer space. We do all of this without so much as batting an eye at the fact that we are constantly operating in a world beyond our natural senses.

How did we get to a point where it is commonplace to communicate through invisible space? This is, after all, the very premise of the most influential space in the world, the tech space - the gatekeeper of the information age and ruler of our modern and future world. But, if we were to step back for a moment and ponder the origins of our tech world and modern communication networks, it stands to reason that the pioneers of this space had to operate at a high level of faith in the unseen, pulling solutions from an invisible world into a physical reality.

The very essence of the tech space points to Hebrews 11:3, "God spoke, and the invisible realm gave birth to all that is seen." And yet, the pervading thought today is that the tech space is an entirely humanistic endeavor, built apart from God. In the modern tech space paradigm, man has replaced God as creator and denied His very existence.

We have to rediscover the origins in order to truly move us forward. What we believe about our origin of existence serves as the foundation upon which we build everything, including technology.

We are at a pivotal moment in how we approach technological advancement and scientific discovery, which have the power to divide us or bring us together as one through an encounter with the love of Christ. It is John 10:10 front and center - the thief has come to steal, kill and destroy; but Jesus has come that we may have abundant life. And it is the Ephesians 6:12 war we wage - not against flesh and blood, but against the principalities, rulers and spiritual hosts of wickedness in the heavenly places.

How we respond will be the key to unlocking the next epoch in science and technology, which I believe will catalyze the next great movement of God. We, the Body of Christ, have to be present. We have to engage instead of retreat so that all will taste and see that the Lord is good. It is the goodness of God that leads men to repentance - not out of compliance or obligation, but from an overwhelming sense of joy of knowing we are all God's children and He created all things in Jesus, on purpose and for relationship with Him.

"For in Him all things were created: things in heaven and on earth, visible and invisible, whether thrones or powers or rulers or authorities; all things have been created through Him and for Him. He is before all things, and in Him all things hold together." (Colossians 1:16-17 NIV)

Or, in the words of Frideswide: whatever is not God is nothing.

1

REDEEMING TECH

"By faith we understand that the worlds were framed by the word of God. He spoke, and the invisible realm gave birth to all that is seen." Hebrews 11:3 TPT

"I'm redeeming the tech space," I heard the Lord say, as I sat in bumper-to-bumper traffic on the San Francisco-Oakland Bay Bridge. I had just finished a meeting with a fortune-level tech company to talk about our new Christian faith-based coding bootcamp, Bethel School of Technology, and I was headed to another major tech company to do the same. The revelation calibrated my heart toward what our mission would be for our school. We weren't just equipping and empowering individuals with in-demand tech skills and high-character values based on Biblical principles; we were called to bring the love of Christ to and through the most influential space in the world.

In 2000, the evangelist Billy Graham prophesied that the next great movement of God would come from believers in the marketplace. What has become evident to me in 15 years of working with companies to support and build their talent acquisition and development goals is that the future of work is in tech. Every company, regardless of industry, is a tech company to some degree, from manufacturing to healthcare. If you want to change the world in the 21st century and beyond, you have to be present within the gates of the space that controls the distribution of information. And the gatekeeper of the information age for all sectors is the tech space.

My pastor at Bethel Church in Redding, CA, Bill Johnson, says it best, "The purest form of influence does not come from invasion; it comes from invitation." Trust is the currency of influence; and in order to establish trust, one must be present. In order to be present in the tech space, one must be equipped with the appropriate language. Bethel School of Technology teaches the language of technology that leads to employment in the marketplace.

In that moment on the Bay bridge I assumed God was saying He was going to graft something into His will that was built apart from Him. I was wrong.

Fast forward to October 2019, about a year later. Again driving, this time to the Sacramento airport from Redding, CA, I heard the Lord ask, "What did you think I meant when I said I'm redeeming the tech space?" I love when He asks questions because, of course, He already knows the answer. I think He asks because His entire point of creating us is for a relationship with Him, and He desires deep, intimate conversations with us. It's from these conversations that we discover solutions to manifest His will on earth as it is in heaven.

We see this in the loaves and fish miracle in John 6:5-10.

As Jesus scanned the hillside and saw the massive crowd falling over themselves to be near Him, He turned to Philip the Disciple, and asked, "Where will we buy enough food to feed these people?" Of course, Jesus already knew the answer, but the question was an opportunity to invite Philip and the rest of the twelve disciples to actively participate in the miracle.

You probably know the rest of the story. Philip told Jesus they didn't have enough money for food to feed the entire crowd. Peter then pointed out a boy who brought five loaves of bread and two fish, and the boy's food offering was more than enough for Jesus to feed the crowd of five thousand, with twelve full baskets leftover.

Jesus is more than able to work with what we have, so long as our hearts are surrendered to what He wants to do and we put our faith into action. When we believe, trust and obey what the Lord is saying, we create an atmosphere for God to move in any situation.

Jesus could have performed the miracle alone. God already set a precedent of raining bread from heaven for the Israelites in the wilderness (Exodus 16:4). But Jesus was doing a new thing. Or better yet, He was restoring the original design of our relationship with Him. Just as the Lord made Adam and Eve to steward creation in partnership with Him, Jesus desired to teach, model and activate His power and authority in the disciples' lives so they could then go and enact His will wherever they went in partnership with His Spirit.

When Jesus asked me what I thought He meant by "redeeming the tech space," I responded to His question by echoing the commonly held belief that the space was a humanistic endeavor built separately from Him. I thought He was grafting it into His plan and purpose to magnify His love to everyone.

The Lord gently corrected me:

> Ryan, when I said I'm redeeming the tech space, I meant that I am regaining possession of something that started with Me so that all would encounter My goodness and love that is beyond natural understanding. The innovation of this space points to My nature as Creator. I take pleasure in My children searching out the beautiful gifts I have in store for them and partnering with them to pull those gifts from heaven to earth.

I was floored by His response, and it piqued my curiosity to discover how and when the Lord partnered with someone to set the foundation of our technological advancements and communication networks that we use today. The Bible says it's the glory of God to conceal a matter, but the glory of kings to search a matter out (Proverbs 25:2). I love the Passion Translation of that verse: "God conceals the revelation of His word in the hiding place of His glory. But the honor of kings is revealed by how they thoroughly search out the deeper meaning of all that God says."

God identifies us as royalty - His children and chosen treasure - to proclaim His goodness as co-heirs with Christ (I Peter 2:9; Romans 8:17). It is, therefore, part of our identity to search and explore the deeper meaning of what God said (and is saying) from glory to glory.

So, I searched. I had to know if there was a particular

moment in history when a believer (or believers) partnered with the Holy Spirit to grab solutions from heaven to earth and create the foundations of our modern technology and communication networks.

To me, it was more than a coincidence that the tech space operated with such a high-level of faith in an invisible realm as its fundamental basis for transferring information from one place to another. The tech space appeared to be a shining example of the second part of Hebrews 11:3, "the invisible realm gave birth to all that is seen." What didn't add up to me was the absence of the first part of the scripture, "By faith we understand that the worlds were framed by the word of God." It was as if there was a veil hiding the part about God speaking the worlds into existence.

How did we get to the point that we could operate in an unseen realm, if we didn't know that it first existed? Unless, of course, a precedent was set in modern science and technology in which humans thought and functioned in a hidden realm to pull unseen ideas and solutions into our natural world.

I found the answer tucked away in mid-19th century Victorian Britain. It was a time and region marked by Divine solutions in science that would change the course of history. And at the center of it all was a Scottish physicist named James Clerk Maxwell, who partnered with the Holy Spirit to materialize God's creativity from an invisible realm into the physical world.

II.

Before we jump into Maxwell's life and discoveries, I'd like to mention a few other notable individuals during this time period. These scientists profoundly shaped the way we live through Holy Spirit-led innovation and paved the way for Maxwell.

There was Charles Babbage (1791-1871), the English mathematician, inventor and mechanical engineer, who is considered the "father of the computer." In the 1830s, Babbage conceived and sketched the blueprint for a machine that would become the forerunner of our modern digital computer over 150 years later. In his autobiography, Babbage, wrote an entire chapter on Divine knowledge and revelation that comes from studying the works of the Creator. In it, he said, regarding the origin of existence:

> In the works of the Creator ever open to our examination, we possess a firm basis on which to raise the superstructure of an enlightened creed. The more man inquires into the laws which regulate the material universe, the more he is convinced that all its varied forms arise from the action of a few simple principles. The works of the Creator, ever present to our senses, give a living and perpetual testimony of his power and goodness far surpassing any evidence transmitted through human testimony. The testimony of man becomes fainter at every stage of transmission, whilst each new inquiry into the works of the Almighty gives to us more exalted views of his wisdom, his goodness, and his power.[2]

On miracles, Babbage wrote:

> We must not measure the credibility or incredibility of an

event by the narrow sphere of our own experience, nor forget that there is a Divine energy which overrides what we familiarly call the laws of nature. All that we see in a miracle is an effect which is new to our observation, and whose cause is concealed. The cause may be beyond the sphere of our observation, and would be thus beyond the familiar sphere of nature; but this does not make the event a violation of any law of nature. The limits of man's observation lie within very narrow boundaries, and it would be arrogance to suppose that the reach of man's power is to form the limits of the natural world.[3]

Babbage understood that observation of the natural world was merely an invitation to discover the miracles of God. In the Bible, miracles are often described as signs and wonders from the superior reality of the kingdom of heaven manifesting into our physical world. The scientific community refers to them as phenomena.

The more we seek to discover those miracles, the more we see the goodness and power of our Creator. To stop at mere observation is to limit ourselves to the confines of our own rationale and deprive ourselves of fully encountering the intent of creation, which is to draw us into a deeper relationship with God.

William Thomson (1824-1907), a.k.a. Lord Kelvin, was another Spirit-led innovator integral to advancement of science and technology during this time. The Scottish engineer, mathematician, and physicist was knighted by Queen Victoria for overseeing the first permanent telegraph line across the Atlantic Ocean, and elected to the Royal Society of London for his work in thermodynamics, absolute temperature scale, and mathematical analysis of electricity and magnetism.* Thomson believed that forces such as electricity, magnetism, and heat were caused by invisible material in motion.[4] His research on electricity and magnetism as a student at Cambridge University greatly influenced Maxwell, who also studied at Cambridge and adopted Thomson as his mentor.[5]

Thomson too was a Creationist. He saw his relationship with God as the inspiration for his scientific work. Take a look at part of his address to the Christian Evidence Society on May 23, 1889:

> I have long felt that there was a general impression in the non-scientific world, that the scientific world believes Science has discovered ways of explaining all the facts of Nature without adopting any definite belief in a Creator. I have never doubted that that impression was utterly groundless. It seems to me that when a scientific man says—as it has been said from time to time—that there is no God, he does not express his own ideas clearly. He is, perhaps, struggling with difficulties; but when he says he does not believe in a creative power, I am convinced he does not faithfully express what is in his own mind, He does not fully express his own ideas. He is out of his depth.
>
> We are all out of our depth when we approach the subject of life. The scientific man, in looking at a piece of dead matter, thinking over the results of certain combinations which he can impose upon it, is himself a

---

*The measurement unit for temperature is called a kelvin in honor of Lord Kelvin.

living miracle, proving that there is something beyond that mass of dead matter of which he is thinking. His very thought is in itself a contradiction to the idea that there is nothing in existence but dead matter. Science can do little positively towards the objects of this society. But it can do something, and that something is vital and fundamental. It is to show that what we see in the world of dead matter and of life around us is not a result of the fortuitous concourse of atoms. [6]

Like Babbage, Thomson viewed the observation of our physical world as an invitation to explore the brilliance of our Creator. His message is a rebuttal to the idea that matter is the result of some random "fortuitous concourse of atoms", which was foundational to the theory of evolution that was rising in prominence during this time period.

And one cannot dive into the life and discoveries of Maxwell, without first mentioning Michael Faraday (1791-1867). Some would say that Faraday entered the scientific community on the cusp of a great enlightenment in how we perceive the physical world. I would propose that Faraday was the spark that produced the flame that ignited a revolution in the world of physics.

The son of a blacksmith, Faraday held a low socioeconomic status, which in Victorian England made it difficult to find opportunity in the world of academia. With no money to fund a college education, Faraday became a bookbinder's apprentice.

The books Faraday helped bind provided an alternative pathway into a world of applied knowledge. He devoured books on science, and committed to pursue a career in studying and discovering the seemingly magical components of electricity.

Over the course of his career, Faraday invented the first electric motor and discovered the chemical benzene. But without question, his greatest achievement was introducing the magnetic field and producing an electric current and magnetic rotation from the magnetic field in what we now call "Faraday induction."[7] This would be the foundation upon which Maxwell would build.

A devout Christian, Faraday believed God was the Creator of everything and the point of origin that unified the forces of magnetism, light and electricity. He gave thanks to the Lord for uncovering the mysteries of the invisible realm, and credited God for bestowing upon him all his gifts and scientific discoveries:

> Yet even in earthly matters I believe that the invisible things of Him from the creation of the world are clearly seen, being understood by the things that are made, even His eternal power and Godhead, and I have never seen anything incompatible between those things of man which can be known by the spirit of man which is within him, and those higher things concerning his future, which he cannot know by that spirit.[8]

Faraday's findings were derived entirely from experimental observation as he had little mathematical training. His non-traditional approach gave him an unmatched understanding of electromagnetism, allowing him to ask questions and see possibilities that others had no grid to ask or think.

This proved to be of great benefit as Maxwell's expertise

lay in mathematical theory, and he was much less-skilled than Faraday in experimentation. The two were like puzzle pieces that fit perfectly together to unlock a hidden mystery in the world of electromagnetism that would change the world forever.

In 1857, Faraday received a copy of a paper titled, "On Faraday's Lines of Force". The author was a young professor at Marischal College, who had written the paper while a student at Cambridge. In it, the author explained his desire to illuminate the importance of Faraday's discoveries in electromagnetic rotations by explaining the findings mathematically. The author was James Clerk Maxwell.

From a very early age, Maxwell was curious about the way the world worked. In a letter to his sister, Maxwell's father said of his then three-year-old son, James:

> He is a very happy man… he has great work with doors, locks, keys, etc., and "Show me how it doos" is never out of his mouth. He also investigates the hidden courses of streams and bell-wires… and he drags papa all over to show him the holes where the wires go through.[9]

That spirit of curiosity would mark Maxwell throughout his life. "Let nothing be left willfully unexamined," he said, describing his approach to science and the universe.[10]

Maxwell (1831-1879) is considered the greatest physicist between Isaac Newton and Albert Einstein. In fact, when Einstein was asked, "Do you stand on the shoulders of Newton," he simply responded, "No, I stand on the shoulders of Maxwell."[11] Einstein also said, "One epoch in science ended and another began with James Clerk

Maxwell."[12]

Why? Because it was Maxwell who ushered in a revolution in the way physicists viewed the natural world. He dared to look at objects and forces in the physical realm as one part of a larger equation, and he believed there had to be an underlying reality, inaccessible by our senses, that could be described mathematically.

Galileo (1564-1642), who is considered the father of observational astronomy and modern physics said that mathematics is the alphabet in which God has written the universe. For Maxwell, it was the underlying invisible reality inexpressible with words that provided further insight into how objects and forces in the physical realm operated and existed.

From this perspective, he discovered mathematically that light was an electromagnetic wave. And, through manipulation of these waves, information could be transferred from one place to the next, even through invisible space.

Maxwell published four equations that formed the foundation of classical electromagnetism, classical optics, and electric circuits. These equations described how electric and magnetic fields are generated by charges and currents, and served as the basis of his law of electrodynamics. His equations were put into application by the German physicist, Heinrich Hertz, in 1886, seven years after Maxwell's death, when Hertz became the first person to transmit and receive controlled radio waves.[13]

Maxwell's discoveries and equations were the start of an epoch of technological advancement that would lead to the great communication networks of today, including radio, television, satellite, mobile phones, electric motors, power generators, and Wi-Fi. These innovations are the fruit of Maxwell's theories of using light to transfer information through space. Like Einstein, our modern tech space stands on the shoulders of Maxwell.

And Maxwell was a Christian, who memorized much of the Bible as a teenager. He believed God and science were not mutually exclusive, but eternally linked - that God the Creator made us in His own image and gave us stewardship over His creation. As such, Maxwell believed that God would reveal His creation to us and with us as we explored the work of His hands. In a lecture at Marischal College, Maxwell said:

Man has indeed but little knowledge of the simplest of God's creatures, the nature of a drop of water has in it mysteries within mysteries utterly unknown to us at present, but what we do know we know distinctly; and we see before us distinct physical truths to be discovered, and we are confident that these mysteries are an inheritance of knowledge, not revealed at once, lest we should become proud in knowledge, and despite patient inquiry, but so arranged that, as each new truth is unraveled it becomes a clear, well-established addition to science, quite free from the mystery which must still remain, to show that every atom of creation is unfathomable in its perfection. While we look down with awe into these unsearchable depths and treasure up with care what with our little line and plummet we can reach, we ought to admire the wisdom of Him who has so arranged these mysteries that we find first that which we can understand at first and the rest in order so that it is possible for us to have an increasing stock of known truth concerning things whose nature is absolutely incomprehensible.[14]

Maxwell viewed the physical world as an invitation to explore the depths of God's goodness. The best gift wasn't the discovery, but rather the intimate relationship and journey-walk with our Creator. The incomprehensible occurrences in nature were an invitation for God to reveal the impossible with us. The discovery was merely the manifestation of the relationship.

Maxwell, Faraday, Babbage, and Thomson, who laid the foundation for the most important elements of our modern technology, understood the invisible realm gave birth to all that is seen, and that it was the work of the Creator, Who causes and sustains both the material and immaterial worlds. This is Hebrews 11:3 actualized.

You would think the tech space, with its high propensity to operate with faith in the invisible realm, would be shouting from the mountaintops that God is Creator and Jesus is King. Yet, what has transpired in the 150 years since the start of Maxwell's epoch doesn't depict a reverence, recognition or relationship with God. At least, that is not what is being taught in the science textbooks from which many of our leading modern technologists have learned.

Rather, the explanation has shifted to a false narrative void of a Creator. On the highway of pulling Divine solutions from the invisible realm to solve problems in the physical world, humankind took a wrong exit, and the consequences have been devastating. In order to appropriately move forward, we must first take a look at where we got off track.

2

THE COUNTERFEIT

"There is a way that seems right to man, but its end is the way of death." Proverbs 14:12 NKJV

Unlike God, Satan does not create. He steals, kills and destroys. Lying is his language, perversion is handiwork, and fear is his weapon of choice.

In the Garden of Eden, the serpent convinced Adam and Eve to believe the lie that God was withholding something good from his children. When in actuality, God was protecting them from the perils of knowing and experiencing sin, which leads to death.

As a parent, this resonates deeply with me. My desire for my children is that they would not experience anything contrary to the goodness of God. I do not need to give my children a taste of avocado ice cream in order for them to fully understand the wondrous splendor of a vanilla ice cream sundae with all the toppings. I only need to give them the real thing to fully experience its goodness.

But God is a loving Father, and He will not force his children to obey Him. Forced obedience is not love. It's tyranny, manifested from the enemy and seeded in a desire to hurt God's treasure—His children. God sets before us life and death, and then implores us to choose life (Deuteronomy 30:15). He implores, but does not force. It is God's desire that none should perish (2 Peter 3:9).

When the devil asked Eve if God said, "You shall not eat of every tree of the garden?" Her response was that she and Adam could eat from all the trees in the garden, except the tree of the knowledge of good and evil.

Then, the devil deceived Eve into thinking she and Adam were being oppressed by God, Who must not have wanted them to be like Him. If they were to eat of the forbidden fruit, *their eyes would be opened* and they, like God, would know all things.

In Ephesians 1:17-21 Paul prays that Jesus would give the church of Ephesus:

> The spirit of wisdom and revelation in the knowledge of Him, the eyes of their understanding being enlightened, that they may know what is the hope of His calling, what are the riches of the glory of His inheritance in the saints, and what is the exceeding greatness of His power toward us who believe, according to the working of His mighty power, which He worked in Christ when He raised him from the dead and seated Him at His right hand in the heavenly places, far above all principality and power and might and dominion, and every name that is named, not only in this age, but also in that which is to come. (NKJV)

The devil tempted Adam and Eve with the opportunity to open their eyes; but, their eyes were already open. The fear of missing out was enough for them to hand over their right-standing in God, who made them in His image and gave them dominion over the earth, including authority over the devil.

Knowledge is an inferior reality to faith. And it is from faith that true knowledge is imparted from God to us through communion relationship with Him.

The enemy could not take authority. He could only be given it through deception.

Whereas the devil presented an invitation to a false sense of enlightenment, Paul prayed for Christ-followers to receive the restoration of our enlightened eyesight of understanding back to its original design through our faith and relationship with Jesus.

How is that possible? It's possible through the working of God's mighty power, which He displayed when He raised Christ from the dead and seated Him at His right hand in the heavenly places, far above all principality and power (Ephesians 1:20-21).

Jesus told the disciples that it would be better that He go be with the Father because He would leave with them His Holy Spirit, who would reside inside of them. They would become as one, and He would unveil the reality of every truth (John 16:13). This is the original enlightenment - that the spirit of the Lord makes His home in the hearts of His children and we make our home in His for eternity.

II.

Richard Feynman is widely considered the greatest American physicist in the field of quantum mechanics since World War

II. In 1964, he said of James Clerk Maxwell, "From a long view of the history of mankind — seen from, say, ten thousand years from now — there can be little doubt that the most significant event of the 19th century will be judged as Maxwell's discovery of the laws of electrodynamics."[15]

The most significant event of the 19th century! Here's what I find amazing about that statement: around the same time Maxwell was publishing his theory and equations on electromagnetism, Charles Darwin was publishing his theory of evolution.

I like to conduct an exercise with our students at Bethel Tech. I'll ask a room of, say, 50 students how many of them have heard of James Clerk Maxwell. Maybe I'll get one hand raised in the room. Then, I'll ask how many of them have heard of Charles Darwin, and all of the students raise their hands. How is it that Darwin is a household name and not Maxwell?

I believe Satan has gone to great lengths to cover up the Divine origin of our existence. In order to do that, he had to first convince humans they were not created by God on purpose; but rather, they were merely the byproduct of an accident billions of years ago—descended from a single cell, then a clump of cells, then a primate, and eventually a human. Satan found his opportunity to deceive mankind in Darwin's theory of evolution, and used it to draw attention away from our loving Father, Who created us in His image.

In 1831, Darwin set sail on a five-year voyage aboard the HMS Beagle to the Galapagos islands, about 620 miles west of the coast of Ecuador. He took particular notice of the differences in the beaks of the island finches. The beaks would change Darwin's view on man's origin of existence, and subsequently set in motion a theory that would become the standardized origin of existence taught in American public schools a century later.

Darwin observed that the beaks of the cactus finches were longer and pointier than the ground finches. And the beaks of the warbler finches were thinner and pointier than both the cactus and ground finches. The shape of the beaks, Darwin inferred, had adapted over time to help the birds better gather available food. According to Darwin, the beaks evolved in order for the birds to survive.[16] Years later, he expanded on this idea and correlated it to all life forms.

In 1859, Darwin wrote his seminal book, *On the Origin of Species by Means of Natural Selection, or the Preservation of Favoured Races in the Struggle for Life*. Or, *Origin of Species*, for short (we'll get to the significance of the full title later).

In his book, Darwin proposed the idea that species have evolved over time to adapt to their environments in order to survive. He based this theory on observation of slight variances in species - most notably, reporting in detail the variations of bird beaks he studied in the Galapagos Island nearly thirty years earlier.

In *Origin of Species,* Darwin attributed God as Creator, as evidenced in the book's concluding sentence:

There is grandeur in this view of life, with its several powers, having been originally breathed by the Creator into a few forms or into one; and that, whilst this planet has gone cycling on according to the fixed law of gravity, from so simple a beginning endless forms most beautiful and most wonderful have been, and are being, evolved.[17]

However, in 1871, twelve years after *Origin of Species,* Darwin published *The Descent of Man, and Selection in Relation to Sex* in which he applied the theory of evolution to human existence and removed God as the source of origin. He pointed to the physical and mental similarities between apes and humans to prove the latter descended from the former, and described religion and morality as being social constructs. Darwin used his observation of "savages," which is what he called uncivilized tribes, as proof that religion is not innate, but rather an outcome of advanced or evolved socialization based on superstition and fetishism, as evidenced in the following passage from *The Descent of Man:*[18]

> Belief in God — Religion. — There is no evidence that man was aboriginally endowed with the ennobling belief in the existence of an Omnipotent God. On the contrary there is ample evidence, derived not from hasty travellers, but from men who have long resided with savages, that numerous races have existed, and still exist, who have no idea of one or more gods, and who have no words in their languages to express such an idea. The question is of course wholly distinct from that higher one, whether there exists a Creator and Ruler of the universe; and this has been answered in the affirmative by some of the highest intellects that have ever existed.[19]

In the book *En-kata: A Time for Singing,* Nadina Feser and photojournalist Jeremy Stephenson brilliantly illuminate the life and culture of the Maasai tribe. Located in the "Bush" of Africa in Tanzania and Kenya, the Maasai are a deeply spiritual people, split between witchcraft and following Jesus.

The Maasai Pastoralists for Evangelism and Development (MAPED) is a group from the tribe who have found freedom and transformation through dramatic encounters with God, and have formed a choir to sing of His love. Through song, they share the freedom, grace, and compassion they've received from Christ to the rest of their community. The choir sings at night because the Maasai evenings have always been filled with music. But what was once a terror-filled concert of warriors singing of their murderous conquests as they chose young girls to have sex with for the night, has now shifted into worship and prayer to God through the voices of the MAPED.

It's incredible how the Word of God transforms lives and dispels the darkness with light. But, perhaps the Word of God is not confined to text written in a book that can only be distributed by man. Below is a fascinating revelation from Feser regarding a woman in the tribe named Sabina, who shared the gospel of Jesus to the rest of the Maasai:

> Up until this point, I had mistakenly assumed that a Western missionary had brought the knowledge of God and Christianity to Lerumo. But Sabina was the first one in the area to hear God, to allow Him to bring change to her life, and to help others to change… This woman who curses the angry warriors and 12-foot pythons in the name of Jesus is, as she calls herself, the mother of the MAPED choir. She is very exuberant in telling her story.

How did Sabina know about Jesus if no missionary had introduced Him to her? One of our Bethel Tech employees, Mark Zapeda, who served as a missionary to the Maasai, shared with me his first-hand experience with the tribe:

> We met Sabina's daughter in person. Through a translator,
> she explained that her mom had initially received an
> audible invitation from God to follow Him. She explained
> that after this [first encounter] followed a series of
> encounters with whom she described to be Jesus. During
> these times she was given an array of teaching that she
> then passed through oral tradition to the people in her
> immediate tribe who would receive it. The Maasai have a
> strong oral tradition which allowed Sabina to capture and
> articulate what had been told to her with ease. When
> Sabina went seeking 'teaching and baptism' and met the
> first Christian missionaries, the missionaries were shocked
> that she had come looking and that she already knew so
> much of the story of Jesus and other biblical elements in
> such great detail, having never encountered the Bible or a
> Christian missionary.

The "savages," as Darwin would have identified them, didn't
need an evolved mental capacity to manufacture a belief
system. Sabina's encounter with Jesus matched the gospels in
the Bible, of which she had never read or heard of from man.
Even if the text of the Bible did not exist, Jesus is the Word,
and He shares His love and testimony to all the ends of the
earth.

Jesus is perfect theology, and He will not be denied His
full reward. All of creation is His full reward and treasure!

But, Darwin was right about one thing: religion is a fraud.
It is a man-made social construct designed to control others
in the name of God. It is the fruit of the pharisaical spirit

Jesus calls a whitewashed tomb in Matthew 23:27 – beautiful on the outside, but full of "dead men's bones and uncleanliness" on the inside, ripe with hypocrisy.

Religion has been the justification for some of the most horrible crimes against humanity in which innocent people have been raped, tortured, mutilated, exiled, murdered, falsely imprisoned, and sold into slavery. It is the insidious spirit that crucified Jesus.

But, the blood of Christ created a new covenant that removed the chasm between Creator and creation. The redeeming love of the Cross is in direct conflict with the lie of religion and its perpetuation of evil.

And belief in God is not religion. It is faith, the substance of things hoped for and evidence of the unseen (Hebrews 11:1). Faith is the foundation of understanding that the worlds were framed by God's voice. It is based on His presence and paramount to an intimate relationship with our Creator, whose Spirit dwells inside of us. It is the testimony of the MAPED. This is what Maxwell understood and Darwin failed to see.

Science, void of the Creator, is merely a religion unto itself. This is the nature of the devil—to worship and elevate oneself above the Creator. And sadly, the lie of evolution has gained influence in all parts of our society, strategically slithering its way into school textbooks as an accepted explanation for the origin of existence.

III.

By the turn of the 20th century, the theory of evolution increased in popularity, first within the scientific community, then with political leaders, and eventually within the education system. In 1925, the highly-publicized court case of *The State of Tennessee vs. John Thomas Scopes* set the topic of evolution on center stage in the United States, pitting the scientific community against Fundamentalist Christians.

Earlier that year, the state of Tennessee passed the Butler Act as a law prohibiting public schools from denying the Biblical account of humankind's origin of existence. Shortly after the law was passed, the American Civil Liberties Union (ACLU) announced that it would fund the case of any teacher who was willing to challenge the law. The ACLU found its test case in John Scopes, a public school teacher who agreed to be arrested for teaching evolution.[20]

The court ruled in favor of Tennessee and the Butler Act, drawing a line in the sand between states that supported the teaching of evolution and those who opposed it. Over the course of the next 30 years, the debate would continue, until 1957, when one event changed everything. The Soviet Union sent Sputnik, the first artificial satellite, into outer space and officially ushered in the start of the U.S.-U.S.S.R. space race.

This was a terrifying turn of events that reverberated across the globe, as it was widely believed the battle for outer space supremacy would be the tipping point for the Cold War. Fearing the U.S. was falling behind the Soviet Union in science and technological innovation, President Dwight D. Eisenhower passed the National Defense Education Act (NDEA) in 1958.

As part of the NDEA, Eisenhower gathered the country's leading biologists to create a science education that could compete with the Soviets. The scientists standardized the theory of evolution as the unifying principle of biology and removed God from humankind's origin story.

One of the most complicated and devastating stumbling blocks in the course of history is when humans replace God's intentions with good intentions. There is a way that seems right to man, but its end is the way of death (Proverbs 14:12).

Since the NDEA took effect over 60 years ago, the U.S. Department of Education has been indoctrinating aspiring technologists with the theory that humans are the fortuitous evolutionary result of an accident 14 billion years ago and not spiritual beings created on purpose by God.

The irony is that the leading innovators and tech companies are not opposed to or unfamiliar with the supernatural. Some of the biggest tech companies in the world will employ psychics to provide them spiritual intel on the future and provide recommendations on where to focus their business efforts. In the survival of the fittest world of the tech space, any channel that provides a leg up on the competition is a channel worth exploring.

I've had psychics reach out to me, who work with some of these companies, wanting to learn more about how Bethel Tech taps into the "spirit realm" and partner with us to provide metaphysical or supernatural solutions for the business world. Although I'm not interested in partnering with or entertaining demonic spirits, this does prove there is a deep curiosity for spiritual solutions in the tech space. The task at hand is to replace the counterfeit of the demonic realm with the superior authority of the kingdom of heaven.

In December 2017 the *New York Times* published the article, "Where Silicon Valley Is Going to Get in Touch with Its Soul." The article describes how high-level executives, from some of the leading tech companies in the world's most influential zip code, unplug from society for extended getaways at New Age retreat centers as they search for ways to detoxify their souls from the burnout of their jobs.

In the article, a former Google product manager states: "There's a dawning consciousness emerging in Silicon Valley as people recognize that their conventional success isn't necessarily making the world a better place. The C.E.O.s, inside they're hurting. They can't sleep at night."

Nowhere in the article does it talk about tech leaders acknowledging Jesus as the solution, or even *a solution*. The drive-by perspective would be to double-down on the narrative that the tech space doesn't want anything to do with Christ.

But, I'll offer up a different point of view. Given that an encounter with the love of Christ is the superior reality that will change one's life and lead people to discover their God-given identities, could it be that Christ-followers need to be more intentional in re-presenting the love of Christ to the tech space in an authentic manner, putting on display the power of the Holy Spirit? What if healings, relational reconciliation, deliverance from mental health issues, and indescribable joy characterized the campuses of the leading tech companies that have such a massive influence on society?

To be clear, there are a number of incredibly bold and loving Christ-followers in the tech space, of whom I have had the privilege of befriending. I'm in awe of their devotion to Jesus and how they navigate situations in which they are often ostracized because of their faith. I've seen them hold themselves above reproach, just as Christ did as He was criticized and slandered by the leaders of his day.

I've watched these Christ-followers rely on the Holy Spirit to guide them in all things and shine the light of God's goodness in the workplace. Because of their high skill and character, they have garnered favor with the leaders of their companies, who have given them space to share the love of Jesus to their colleagues. They are modern-day Esthers, Daniels, and Josephs. We need more of these courageous individuals in the most influential sphere in the world!

I had one high-level executive at a major tech company, who is a Christian, tell me he dreams of healings breaking out at his company that have no other explanation other than the love of Jesus. And, he has started partnering with the Holy Spirit to plant seeds of revival in the tech space!

He shared a story with me about a woman in one of his executive meetings, who mentioned that she was losing hearing in her ear. After the meeting, he asked her if he could pray for her. She agreed, thinking he meant that he would pray for her on his own at home. But he prayed for her on the spot, declaring in the name of Jesus full restoration of hearing in her ear. The next morning, he received a text from the woman, stating that his prayer had worked and her hearing had been restored!

My friend Nona Jones was the head of global faith-based partnerships at Meta/Facebook. We first met a few years ago when she was working on an initiative to expand the walls of the church by using Facebook community groups to provide a digital platform for church community services.

Interestingly enough, Nona's role existed because of how well faith-based communities leverage Facebook to help people and build community. When Facebook launched their community groups platform and started analyzing the data from it, they found faith-based organizations had the highest level of engagement. Furthermore, the data revealed that the online engagement among faith-based community groups would often lead to high in-person engagement. The excellence of the church in building community was attractive for one of the leading tech companies in the world, and it became a model to replicate for other community groups. Nona stewarded her role with excellence and brought high-level executives to church, some of whom had never been to a church service before Nona invited them.

At just over 29 thousand feet above sea level, Mount Everest is the highest mountain in the world. Scientists have aptly named Everest's elevation above 26 thousand feet the "death zone" because oxygen is so limited at this height that the human body's cells start to die. Without appropriate oxygen, a climber's judgment becomes impaired and the body begins to shut down. Any prolonged period of time not connected to a source of oxygen in the death zone, and climbers will experience heart attacks, strokes or severe altitude sickness that can lead to death.

As humans climb the proverbial mountain of human intellect apart from God, they find the higher they go without tapping into the true source of creation's origin, the harder it is to survive. The leaders of the most influential space in the world are getting stuck in the "death zone" and looking for the way of life.

We are living in a season of intense desperation to find the true source of life, even if those who have found themselves in the death zone don't yet realize it. Desperation often creates a strong sense of hunger and humility. And hunger and humility are the spiritual ingredients that soften one's heart to receive Jesus, Who is the Way, Truth and Life.

The leading innovators of our day are using (with excellence) the gifts and talents God placed in their lives and operating with a high-level of faith in an invisible realm. And yet, they limit themselves because they have not enlightened the eyes of their understanding. They are like Nicodemus, who could not yet see the Kingdom of God. But the good news is, Nicodemus eventually did, and I believe the same is true for the great modern and future innovators of our day.

In Acts 17, we find the Apostle Paul's presentation of the gospel in Athens, Greece, which, like Silicon Valley, was an epicenter of human intellect at that time. Paul saw all of the idol statues to the Greek gods, and he was provoked by the Holy Spirit to bring the truth of Jesus to the city.

After sharing the good news of Jesus in the synagogue and marketplace, the leading philosophers brought him to a high council of elders, the Areopagus, to share his ideas of Jesus and the resurrection, of which they had never heard.

Paul addresses the Areopagus, not by condemning their belief in other gods, but by honoring their curiosity in and reverence for the spirit realm, "perceiving that in all things they were very religious." Particularly, he pointed to the statue "TO THE UNKNOWN GOD" and saw it as his common ground, or open door, to share the testimony of Jesus:

For as I was passing through and considering the objects of your worship, I even found an altar with this inscription: TO THE UNKNOWN GOD. Therefore, the One whom you worship without knowing, Him I proclaim to you: "God, who made the world and everything in it, since He is Lord of heaven and earth, does not dwell in temples made with hands. Nor is He worshiped with men's hands, as though He needed anything, since He gives to all life, breath, and all things. And He has made from one blood every nation of men to dwell on all the face of the earth, and has determined their preappointed times and the boundaries of their dwellings, so that they should seek the Lord, in the hope that they might grope for Him and find Him, though He is not far from each one of us; for in Him we live and move and have our being, as also some of your own poets have said, 'For we are also His offspring.'

Therefore, since we are the offspring of God, we ought not to think that the Divine Nature is like gold or silver or stone, something shaped by art and man's devising. Truly, these times of ignorance God overlooked, but now commands all men everywhere to repent, because He has appointed a day on which He will judge the world in righteousness by the Man whom He has ordained. He has given assurance of this to all by raising Him from the dead. (Acts 17:23-31 NKJV)

Because of Paul's boldness to share the good news of Jesus in an unfamiliar space, the gospel was deposited in one of the most influential cities in the world. After Paul's sermon to the Areopagus, one of the council's members, Dionysius, became a Christ-follower. As a result, it is believed that Dionysius became the first Bishop of the first church in Athens.* The

---

* Another account says that he went with Paul to Rome, and then was sent by St. Clement, Bishop of Rome, to preach the Gospel in France, eventually becoming the Bishop of France.

Kingdom of God was expanded in the most advanced, intellectual, and (perhaps) influential society of the day - all because Paul, an ambassador of Christ, was present and had the boldness to share his testimony of Jesus.

A lie is like a cancer that spreads and destroys anything it contacts. The lie of evolution spreads its destructive tentacles throughout humanity because deception is the native tongue of the devil. The fruits of the Holy Spirit are love, joy, peace, patience, kindness, goodness, faithfulness, gentleness, and self-control (Galatians 5:22-23). But the fruit of the enemy is deception, death and destruction.

We cannot compartmentalize the consequences of a counterfeit origin strictly to science because it infiltrates everything we do, including how we treat others. If our existence is birthed from an accident, then we as humanity are in a perpetual state of trying to fix ourselves.

If humans are on this planet by some random fortuitous concourse of atoms, void of purpose, and life is a zero-sum, survival-of-the-fittest game, then people can validate approaching other people as competition and seeing individuals or people-groups different from themselves as mistakes.

This is the opposite of our core belief as a Christ-follower. The Word of God says we are all fearfully and wonderfully made by God (Psalm 139:14). His Word says that He created our inmost being and knew us before He knit us together in the womb (Jeremiah 1:5). Our hope is in His son Jesus, Whom He sent to us, so that all who believe in Him shall not perish, but will have everlasting life (John 3:16).

Let's go back to the Scopes Monkey Trial, to which it is commonly referred. Scopes was teaching from a book called

A Civic Biology: Presented in Problems, published in 1914. I want to take a moment to share with you some excerpts from the book.

"Evolution of Man" – Undoubtedly there once lived upon the earth races of men who were much lower in their mental organization than the present inhabitants. If we follow the early history of man upon the earth, we find that at first he must have been little better than one of the lower animals. He was a nomad, wandering from place to place, feeding upon whatever living things he could kill with his hands. Gradually he must have learned to use weapons, and thus kill his prey, first using rough stone implements for this purpose. As man became more civilized, implements of bronze and of iron were used. About this time the subjugation and domestication of animals began to take place. Man then began to cultivate the fields, and to have a fixed place of abode other than a cave. The beginnings of civilization were long ago, but even to-day the earth is not entirely civilized.[21]

"The Races of Man" – At the present time there exist upon the earth five races or varieties of man, each very different from the other in instincts, social customs, and, to an extent, in structure. These are the Ethiopian or negro type, originating in Africa; the Malay or brown race, from the islands of the Pacific; The American Indian; the Mongolian or yellow race, including the natives of China, Japan, and the Eskimos; and finally, the highest type of all, the caucasians, represented by the civilized white inhabitants of Europe and America.[22]

"Improvement of Man" – If the stock of domesticated animals can be improved, it is not unfair to ask if the health and vigor of the future generations of men and women on the earth might not be improved by applying to them the laws of selection. This improvement of the future race has a number of factors in which we as individuals may play a part. These are personal hygiene, selection of healthy mates, and the betterment of the environment.[23]

"Eugenics" – When people marry there are certain things that the individual as well as the race should demand. The most important of these is freedom from germ diseases which might be handed down to the offspring. Tuberculosis, syphilis, that dread disease which cripples and kills hundreds of thousands of innocent children, epilepsy, and feeble-mindedness are handicaps which it is not only unfair but criminal to hand down to posterity. The science of being well born is called eugenics.[24]

"Parasitism and its Cost to Society" – Hundreds of families such as those described above exist today, spreading disease, immorality, and crime to all parts of this country. The cost to society of such families is very severe. Just as certain animals or plants become parasitic on other plants or animals, these families have become parasitic on society. They not only do harm to others by corrupting, stealing, or spreading disease, but they are actually protected and cared for by the state out of public money. Largely for them the poorhouse and the asylum exist.

They take from society, but they give nothing in return. They are true parasites.[25]

"The Remedy" – If such people were lower animals, we would probably kill them off to prevent them from spreading. Humanity will not allow this, but we do have the remedy of separating the sexes in asylums or other places and in various ways preventing intermarriage and the possibilities of perpetuating such a low and degenerate race. Remedies of this sort have been tried successfully in Europe and are now meeting with some success in this country.[26]

What I just outlined, quoting directly from *A Civic Biology*, is the blueprint of Satan's false narrative for our origin of existence. First, the lie is introduced that humankind was not created by God. Instead, we evolved over billions of years from an accident. Proof is found, in part, by observing "savage civilizations" that have yet to advance past the "lower mental organization" of our ancestors from which we evolved.

Second, the lie spreads to create a paradigm of fear and control. With evolution, this manifests in a hierarchy of races, and becomes easy to validate because once people remove God the Creator out of the equation, we subsequently remove the truth of "Imago Dei" - that we were all made in His image and are equal in His sight.

According to this worldview, we have a "Preservation of Favoured Races in the Struggle for Life," as the full title of Darwin's *Origin of Species* states. Some races evolve and advance faster than others, with the lower races holding back the favored races from advancing at an optimum rate.

Next, the lie puts life and death in the hands of the superior races, by introducing the idea that there is a way to perpetuate the desirable characteristics of the favored races and remove people of less desirable races, traits, and physical or mental capacity. This is the science of eugenics, which proposes that through breeding, we can manufacture the desirable heritable characteristics of offspring in order to improve future generations and breed out the "parasites" of humanity, to quote directly from the text. Inevitably, eugenics pits life against life in a zero-sum game for survival in an effort to protect the greater good of the desired races by any means necessary, including death.

Francis Galton, who was Darwin's half-cousin, is considered the father of eugenics. He took Darwin's theory of evolution as a foundation to justify the weeding out of humans he considered to be parasites to society.

And the remedy? According to *A Civic Biology*, humans, like the lower animals, would kill off the "low and degenerate races". But given humanity's social construction of compassion, the workaround is a slow covert extinction by means of forced sterilization, abortion, infanticide, and euthanasia. Ultimately, these paths that seem so logical lead humanity toward genocide in the name of science.

IV.

After World War I, a growing number of scientists and political leaders supported eugenics, including Adolf Hitler, the leader of Nazi party in Germany. A.E. Wilder Smith (1915-1995), who was a British organic chemist and creationist, wrote that one of the pillars of Nazi doctrine was an evolutionary theory that called for the eradication of less evolved races through political measures.[27]

Eugenics served as the foundation for Hitler's obsession to develop a superior thoroughbred race and exterminate all other inferior races and people-groups. As a result, 11 million people (including six million Jews) were killed during the Holocaust because they posed a threat to the rise of a superior, evolutionarily-advanced Aryan race.

A common thread connecting the world's most oppressive and murderous dictators over the last 150 years is their belief in evolution and admiration for Darwin. They used "survival of the fittest" as a way to validate the mass genocide of what they believed to be inferior people groups. The following is a brief overview of some of these dictators, and the death, destruction, hate and evil propagated in the name of Darwinism.

Adolf Hitler (1889-1945), the aforementioned leader of the Nazi Party and Holocaust architect, based his racial and social policies on the evolutionary ideas of survival of the fittest and the "preservation of the favored races in the struggle for life." During his rule, over 11 million Jews, Black people, gypsies, mentally and physically handicapped, and other groups deemed unfit to live were murdered in the name of eugenics.

Vladimir Lenin (1870-1924) was the founder and first Prime Minister of the Russian Communist Party, as well as the architect and first head of the Soviet State. Lenin was a great admirer of Darwin, as was his mentor, Karl Marx, who is considered the father of Communism. In his office Lenin had a statue of an ape sitting on a pile of books looking at a human skull. One of the books was *Origin of Species*, and the statue was a nod to the Darwinian ideology that man evolved from brute apes, individual lives were inconsequential, and only the fittest humans would survive and advance toward the future. Lenin was responsible for an estimated 3 million deaths during his rule.

Mao Zedong (1893-1976) also known as "Chairman Mao," was the founding father of the Communist People's Republic of China. His regime was responsible for the deaths of as many as 80 million victims through starvation, persecution, concentration camps, and mass executions. Convinced that "without the continual pressure of natural selection" humans would degenerate, Zedong regarded Darwinism as the foundation of China's scientific and political ideologies.[28]

Joseph Stalin (1878-1953) ruled the Soviet Union from 1924 to 1953, and ordered the killing of an estimated 60 million people during his reign. A theology student at Orthodox Spiritual Seminary in Tiflis, Stalin abandoned his faith in God after reading Darwin's theory of evolution. He used evolution as license to torture and murder freely since, according to Darwin, conscience and morals were social constructs. He is said to have "killed with a coldness that even Hitler might have envied—and in even greater numbers than Hitler did."[29]

A childhood friend of Stalin said of Darwin's influence on the dictator's worldview:

We youngsters had a passionate thirst for knowledge.

Thus, in order to disabuse the minds of our seminary students of the myth that the world was created in six days, we had to acquaint ourselves with the geological origin and age of the earth, and be able to prove them in argument; we had to familiarize ourselves with Darwin's teachings. We were aided in this by . . . Lyell's *Antiquity of Man* and Darwin's *Descent of Man*, the latter in a translation edited by Sechenov. Comrade Stalin read Sechenov's scientific works with great interest. We gradually proceeded to a study of the development of class society, which led us to the writings of Marx, Engels and Lenin. In those days the reading of Marxist literature was punishable as revolutionary propaganda... The first thing we had to do, he would say, was to become atheists. Many of us began to acquire a materialist outlook and to ignore theological subjects. Our reading in the most diverse branches of science not only helped our young people to escape from the bigoted and narrow-minded spirit of the seminary, but also prepared their minds for the reception of Marxist ideas. Every book we read, whether on archaeology, geology, astronomy, or primitive civilization, helped to confirm us the truth of Marxism.[30]

After the world saw the horrifying atrocities committed by the Nazi's in the name of building a superior race in the 1930s and 1940s, the science community at large in the West distanced itself from the field of eugenics. But the history of evil is destined to repeat itself unless the root lie is exposed and replaced with the truth. And so, the destructive fruits of eugenics continue to permeate culture today, as the flywheel of evil gains steam.

3

IN THE NAME OF SCIENCE

"Woe to those who call evil good, and good evil; who put darkness for light, and light for darkness." Isaiah 5:20 NKJV

In 1921, Margaret Sanger founded the American Birth Control League which would later become Planned Parenthood, a women's clinic that advocates for and employs doctors to perform abortions.[31] Planned Parenthood has become the leading voice in the pro-abortion movement. The organization's revenue is over $1.6 billion per year, of which 95% comes from abortion services.[32]

Since 1973, when the United States Supreme Court legalized abortions via *Roe vs. Wade*, over 63 million unborn babies have been murdered in the name of choice and science. That is nearly six times more deaths than Hitler and the Nazis were responsible for during the Holocaust.

Sanger, who died in 1966, was a proponent of eugenics, particularly as it related to what she deemed "inferior races." Sanger believed that she was "working in accord with the universal law of evolution."[33]

Specifically, she thought the brains of Black people and

Jews were more-closely related to the brains of apes than of white people. She wrote:

> The lower down in the scale of human development we go the less sexual control we find. It is said the aboriginal Australian, the lowest known species of the human family, just a step higher than the chimpanzee in brain development, has so little sexual control that police authority alone prevents him from obtaining sexual satisfaction on the streets. According to one writer, the rapist has just enough brain development to raise him above the animal, but like the animal, when in heat, knows no law except nature, which impels him to procreate, whatever the result.[34]

Sanger often credited Darwin for inspiring her ideology around (what she called) de-selecting the "unfit" people of society from the future of civilization. This de-selection (or extermination) process of the mentally and physically unfit, impoverished, and inferior races, included euthanasia, forced sterilization, selective breeding, and abortion.

Regarding the elimination of the "inferior" non-white races, Sanger promoted a "race betterment" program that strategically placed abortion clinics in non-white communities. In a journal entry, Sanger praised and championed Hitler's "final solution" to "create a race of thoroughbreds."

She opened her first clinic in 1916 in the impoverished Brownsville section of Brooklyn, NY, home to the "immigrant Europeans and Jews" she wished to eliminate.[35] And in 1930, she opened a clinic in Harlem to target the

Black and Latino communities.[36]

Sanger believed the Black community was the headquarters for the "criminal element", and the future of the white race depended upon the elimination of people of color.[37] She was a keynote speaker at a women's Ku Klux Klan rally in New Jersey where she touted birth control as a way to eliminate the inferior races.[38] And in 1939, she developed the "Negro Project" in which she recruited Black doctors, nurses, pastors and social workers to gain the Black community's trust to accept abortion as an acceptable form of reproductive healthcare.[39]

In a letter to fellow eugenicist Clarence Gamble, who was the heir to Proctor and Gamble, Sanger wrote, "We do not want word to go out that we want to exterminate the Negro population, and the minister is the man who can straighten out that idea if it ever occurs to any of their more rebellious members."[40]

Today, over a century later from its inception, Planned Parenthood is the leading abortion provider in the U.S., and is responsible for nearly 1,000 abortions every day. According to Students for Life, Planned Parenthood performs 81 abortions for every adoption referral and 35 abortions for every prenatal care service it provides.[41] In 2021, the organization received over 633 million in taxpayer dollars.[42]

Additionally, Planned Parenthood clinics continue to be disproportionately located in people of color neighborhoods. Between 2012-2016, there were 18,299 more Black babies aborted than live births in New York City.[43] During that same time, births among whites, Asian and Hispanic communities in New York City far surpassed abortions. Currently, there are nearly 2,000 Black babies aborted every day.[44]

A 2011 study revealed that Planned Parenthood facilities were located in zip codes that were more than two and a half times as likely to be disproportionately Black and/or Hispanic communities.[45] And a 2004 study showed that 38.2 percent of abortions in the U.S. were performed on Black women, who make up 12.5 percent of the female population.[46] The abortion rate for Black people is nearly four times as high as it is for non-Black people.

The hopes, dreams, plans and purposes of all humankind are being annihilated in the name of a perverse faux compassion and freedom of choice. This is what happens when society believes and accepts that our origin of existence comes from an accidental occurrence. It is the consequence of the idea that we evolved from a clump of cells. It is much easier to justify removing a clump of cells than murdering a baby.

In April 2021, Planned Parenthood President and CEO Alexis McGill Johnson wrote an Op-ed in *The New York Times* titled, "We're done Making Excuses for Our Founder." In it, she quasi-denounces Sanger for her racist ideology and attempts to distance the organization from the views of its founder, and at the same time still makes excuses for Planned Parenthood's founder being a product of the season. Planned Parenthood goes into further explanation on its website:

Whether our founder was a racist is not a simple yes or no question. Our reckoning is understanding her full legacy, and its impact. Our reckoning is the work that comes next. And the first step is making Margaret Sanger less prominent in our present and future.

Sanger remains an influential part of our history and

will not be erased, but as we tell the history of Planned
Parenthood's founding, we must fully take responsibility
for the harm that Sanger caused to generations of people
with disabilities and Black, Latino, Asian-American, and
Indigenous people.[47]

To take full responsibility for Sanger's racist and eugenicist
ideology would be to acknowledge that Planned Parenthood
is the direct manifestation of Sanger's racist and eugenicist
ideology, of which there is no ambiguity. Johnson distancing
Planned Parenthood from Sanger is a self-preservation tactic
to protect her organization from being culture-canceled for
its racist origins and mission. To this point, the organization
would appear to have immunity from the cancel mob, even
though it has been directly responsible for the suppression of
the Black population in the United States.

The dehumanization of the unborn points right back to
the lies set in motion by Darwin and Galton. With over 63
million babies murdered to date, abortion affects all of
humanity because at its core it seeks to eliminate human life.
Sanger's "Negro Project" is a prime example of Planned
Parenthood's nefarious roots to steal, kill and destroy what
they deem the "unfit" of society.

God is no respecter of persons; we are all His heart's
desire. Conversely, Satan is also no respecter of persons; we
are all disposable in his eyes.

The narrative today coming from the abortion industry is a
repurposed form of eugenics disguised as choice and
compassion. And it has paved the way for sophisticated
genocide— all in the name of science.

II.

Dr. James Watson and Dr. Francis Crick won the Nobel peace prize in 1962 for their discoveries of double helix structure of DNA molecule and its significance for information transfer in living material. Among other things, their discoveries have been instrumental in the advancement of prenatal testing. They also happen to be two of the most ardent eugenicists of the last 50 years, advocating for the practice of infanticide. Watson stated:

> If a child were not declared alive until three days after birth, then all parents could be allowed the choice only a few are given under the present system. The doctor could allow the child to die if the parents so choose and save a lot of misery and suffering. I believe this view is the only rational, compassionate attitude to have.[48]

Likewise, Crick reasoned, "No newborn infant should be declared human until it has passed certain tests regarding its genetic endowment, and that if it fails these tests it forfeits the right to live."[49] Failure to pass these tests meant the infant was merely a clump of cells, and not human.

Crick also believed that society could systematically weed out the "unfit" over time by licensing only the fit people of society to have children. He recommended a child tax in order to curb the number of children born into low-income families.

Generally, there are three main areas of prenatal diagnosis—to detect any problems with the mother or baby's health during pregnancy; to give parents time to prepare in the event a health problem or disability is detected; and to give the parents a chance to abort the baby upon detection of an issue.

I do not want to discount the benefits of prenatal testing. However, in combination with the option to abort a baby, the consequences are leading humanity into a dark, morbid ditch of destruction.

For example, Down syndrome was one of the first genetic conditions to be screened for in utero, and it has become a point of emphasis with prenatal testing. Over the past 30 years there has been a concerted effort to eliminate babies with detected Down syndrome in the womb. Scientists have found themselves in a moral conundrum when it comes to screening for Down syndrome because it is the easiest condition to detect in the womb, leading many parents to abort babies upon diagnosis. Yet, the genetic condition of Down syndrome is very much compatible with a long, happy life.

In December of 2020 *The Atlantic* published an article titled "The Last Children of Down Syndrome" by Sarah Zhang. It's a gut-wrenching look into how Denmark has all but eliminated the future existence of people with Down syndrome, and how other first-world countries, including the U.S., are starting to follow suit.

In 2004, Denmark began offering prenatal Down syndrome screening to all pregnant women in the country. Nearly all expectant mothers choose to take the test. Of those who receive a Down syndrome diagnosis, nearly all (over 95 percent) choose to abort. In 2019, there were only 18 babies with Down syndrome babies born in Denmark. In the United States the abort rate after Down syndrome diagnosis is 67 percent.

The main interviewee in the article is Grete Fält-Hansen, a 54-year-old schoolteacher, who also heads up the National Down Syndrome Association in Denmark. Sitting next to Fält-Hansen in the interview is her 18-year-old son, Karl Emil, who has Down syndrome.

As Zhang and his mother talk about the reality of prenatal testing leading to the eventual elimination of people like himself, Karl Emil's mood takes a somber shift. Zhang writes:

> At one point, Grete was reminded of a documentary that had sparked an outcry in Denmark. She reclaimed her phone to look up the title: Død Over Downs ("Death to Down Syndrome"). When Karl Emil read over her shoulder, his face crumpled. He curled into the corner and refused to look at us. He had understood, obviously, and the distress was plain on his face.

"He must be aware of the debate?" Zhang asked Karl Emil's mother. "So he's aware there are people who don't want people like him to be born?" "Yes," his mother replied.

This is the evolution of eugenics—evil repeating itself in sophisticated ways according to the advancements of the current society. It is human beings believing the lie they originated from an accident, treating other human beings as such in a quest to evolve into a perfect species.

In her article, Zhang writes that eugenics has a history in Denmark. Albeit less militant that Nazi Germany in the 1930s, it shares the same underlying purpose—to create a thoroughbred race by preventing the birth of the "unfit."

In the 1970s, when Denmark began offering prenatal testing to women, the narrative centered around the context of saving the cost it takes to care for or institutionalize a child with a disability. In 1994, the narrative shifted to a woman's right to choose what she does with her body. Although "choice" was the commonly accepted position among the healthcare and scientific communities, the recommended course of action from doctors, who deliver the prenatal test results showing a genetic condition, was to abort the child. A perceived expert opinion goes a long way in persuading one's choice.

In January 2022, *The New York Times* published a report on the inaccuracy of nascent prenatal tests that look for microdeletions, which are small missing snippets of chromosomes. The analysis showed that positive results are incorrect about 85 percent of the time. As a result of the false positives, women have chosen to abort their babies.[50]

Scientists tout the high efficacy of prenatal testing for Down syndrome as a springboard to create and offer additional prenatal tests for genetic disabilities. And the pharmaceutical companies are moving at rapid speed to create new tests that detect rare genetic conditions. Analysts estimate the market size for new genetic condition tests ranges from $600 million into the billions, and the number of women taking these tests is projected to double by 2025.

But a big reason the market is exploding is the projected demand for parents to create designer babies through preimplantation genetic selection (PGT) of embryos via in vitro fertilization (IVF). Currently with PGT, parents can test for rare and severe genetic conditions, such as cystic fibrosis, and choose which embryos to implant in the womb. The next iteration of PGT points to identifying more common, livable conditions, such as diabetes and high cholesterol.

The pie-in-the-sky opportunity for big pharma is the opportunity to charge parents through the roof for the luxury of flipping through desired physical and mental traits of their babies like home buyers combing through swatches to determine the best color of paint for their walls. In his book *Brief Answers to Big Questions*, renowned physicist and futurist Stephen Hawking expressed his concern that in the near future wealthy people will be able to edit their children's DNA to create a superhuman species. He wrote: "Once superhumans appear, there will be significant political problems with unimproved humans who will be unable to compete." He added, "Presumably, they will die out, or become unimportant. Instead there will be a race of self-designing beings who are improving at an ever-increasing rate."[51]

It's what Rosemarie Garland-Thomson, a bioethicist and professor emerita at Emory University, whom Zhang interviewed for her *Atlantic* article, calls the commercialization of reproduction "velvet eugenics." First, for its "soft, subtle way it encourages the eradication of disability." And second, for the way it turns people into products as consumers get to pick the "velvet" premium-tier traits of their future children.

I share this not as a political statement, although I recognize the political sphere is the first place society compartmentalizes this issue, and governmental laws do impact how we live. I share this because the idea of picking and choosing who gets to live and die, born and unborn, did not happen by coincidence, nor did it happen overnight. This is and has been a deliberate weapon from the enemy to steal, kill and destroy God's most beloved treasure - His children - by strategically removing God out of the origin story over time.

True compassion comes from our loving Father because it's in His nature. Because He made us in His image, it is part of our nature as well.

I love what Nelson Mandela said, "No one is born hating another person because of the color of his skin, or his background, or his religion. People must learn to hate, and if they can learn to hate, they can be taught to love, for love comes more naturally to the human heart than its opposite."[52]

But any compassion void of truth is perversion. It is manipulation to coerce others to achieve a self-serving agenda.

What we accept to be true will inevitably lead how we live our lives. The further we get from the truth, the more irrational it seems. The further we go down the road of a lie, the more difficult it is to recognize its error.

Science will always seek to affirm the belief system of those who control it. Technology is a tool that takes on the function of its user.

We default to the expert opinions of leaders in science and technology because we are living in a society which they have created and rule. And the experts have been indoctrinated with the lie of evolution. In their minds, it's a no-brainer that we originated from an accident billions of years ago. If there is no God, then we get to play god, and technology is then built and used to validate what we believe and what we decide is best for humanity.

Abortion, eugenics, infanticide, and anything that promotes the elimination of people is pure evil straight from the pit of hell. But, it is important to understand there are well-intentioned people who sincerely believe abortion is helping people. If all you've been exposed to is a counterfeit version of the truth, it becomes your truth by default. We can't get caught up in a battle against flesh and blood because all people were made in God's image. We do however war against the spiritual hosts of wickedness in the heavenly places that have cast a veil over the eyes of well-intentioned people.

We have a responsibility to stand up for and protect the vulnerable, including unborn babies, marginalized and oppressed people-groups, human-trafficking victims, labor slaves, and any other person or group being intentionally hurt and exploited. We do this through prayer, coming against the demonic powers in the heavenly places, and mobilizing and partnering with individuals and organizations committed to eradicating these atrocities.

We do this with our purchasing power. Choosing to boycott companies that have chosen to partner with any group that hurts and exploits the vulnerable is a powerful way to put an end to the industry of evil. When demand goes away, so too does the supply.

We also do this in the political space. In June 2022, The U.S. Supreme Court eliminated the constitutional right to abortion in the landmark case, *Dobbs vs. Jackson Women's Health Organization*. The Court's decision overturned *Roe vs. Wade,* and was a giant leap in the fight to protect the inherent right to life for all Americans, born and unborn, as described in the 14th Amendment of the U.S. Constitution.

But there is still much work to be done. The Supreme Court's decision gave each state the power to pass pro-life or pro-abortion laws, and pro-abortion states and corporations within those states are going on the attack.

A number of companies have added abortion travel cost reimbursement as an employee benefit.[53] And the state of California's marketing department launched a billboard campaign in seven of the top pro-life states in the country, with a message that doctors at California health care facilities will gladly perform abortions for women in pro-life states. One billboard that California ran in Texas quoted Mark 12:31, "Love your neighbor as yourself. There is no other greater commandment greater than these."[54] I can't help but be reminded that even the devil quoted scripture when he tempted Jesus in the wilderness.

The eternal solution, however, is not to condemn, but to convict people of righteousness and lead them into an encounter with Jesus. We know that, through one encounter with the love of Christ, we can discover our God-given identity as His sons and daughters. One encounter with Jesus will expose the lies and replace them with the One who is Truth and Who enters every person's heart who lets Him in.

When I was in my late twenties and just getting into the corporate world I met someone who exemplified what it looks like to convict people of righteousness in the abortion debate, and his testimony forever marked my life. At the time, Briana and I were attending a weekly Equip class at Gateway Church in Southlake, TX hosted by Melody and Steve Dulin.

From the first time I met Steve, I aspired to be like him. He didn't just talk about following Jesus, but he walked it out in the marketplace.

One particular story he shared opened up my eyes to what it looks like to partner with the Holy Spirit in the workplace, going beyond business plans and balance sheets. Before Steve became a pastor at Gateway, he owned a successful commercial construction company in the Dallas-Fort Worth area. You can hear the full details of the story in Steve's audio series, "Masterplan," but I will summarize it, focusing on the area that most impacted me.

Steve had a potential client who wanted his company to build a facility on a large plot of land. The client asked him to meet her at the location of the future building site. Steve met with the client, and she shared that she wanted him to build tall security walls around the structure and metal bars on the windows.

As she was talking, Steve realized she was describing an abortion clinic, and he asked her if that was the purpose of the building. It was, and she apologized for not being upfront with him. She said she always tells people what she does before entering into a business relationship because of the sensitivity of her work, and couldn't believe she failed to tell him as well. I believe this was a Divine set-up, and not an accidental oversight.

Steve told her he was pro-life, and could not build the facility. Faced with a crossroads of what to do next, Steve leaned into what the Holy Spirit was asking him to do. Instead of walking away and blasting this woman for her sin to his circle of friends, Steve engaged the woman as God saw her—His daughter, whom He loved deeply.

Steve then spoke what God was saying to him about her. He started by recognizing her heart to do what is right. Steve honored her for her attempt to help people based on her belief that she was saving lives. He went on to say that God sees her heart and He wants to show her what she thought was right was actually counter to His love and plan for His children.

Then, Steve asked the woman if he could pray with her. Thinking he meant that he would pray for her on his own time, she said "yes". Much to her surprise, Steve prayed for her on the spot. He prayed that God would tell her how He sees her, expose the lie she had been believing, convict her of righteousness, and reveal His plan for her life.

When Steve opened his eyes, he saw tears streaming down the woman's face. She said she had encountered many Christians throughout her career. They would call her names, cuss her out, spit at her, and condemn her to hell. But he was the first Christian, who actually saw her as a human being and took the time to pray with her.

Isn't it ironic that the Christians who were attacking her because she failed to see the life inside a womb as a human being– God's treasure– were treating her as something less than God's child outside of the womb. Repaying sin with sin doesn't produce righteousness. It only perpetuates more sin. If a person encounters us as Christians and doesn't encounter the love of Jesus, we haven't done our job.

Steve gave the woman his cell phone number, and said she could talk to him and his wife whenever she needed. When he went home and told his wife what had happened, she recognized the woman as the leading pro-choice advocate in the Dallas-Fort Worth area.

Over the next few weeks, the woman would call Steve, and he and his wife would pray for her. Then, she went silent.

About six months later, Steve looked at the front page of the *Fort Worth Star-Telegram* Metro section, and the main headline read something to the effect of, "Leading Pro-

THE GOD OF TECH

Choice Advocate Steps Down." The article went on to explain that the woman walked away from the industry because she believed that abortion was wrong; and what she thought she was doing to help people was actually hurting them.

Because Steve did not condemn this woman to hell like so many of the other Christians she had encountered in her past, she was moved to repentance. Because he spoke to the righteousness that is embedded in her DNA as a child of God, and he saw her as God's treasure worthy of the price of the blood of the Lamb, she was receptive to listening to who God said she was.

From that moment on, I vowed to be like Steve. I wanted to bring Jesus to everyone I encountered, so that they might encounter the love of Christ and enter into a personal relationship with Him. My mission was to stand firm in not condoning sin, and convict people of the righteousness and purpose bestowed upon them from the Lord.

Since then, I have had a number of conversations with, and prayed for, individuals who either were strong abortion advocates or themselves had an abortion. In one particular instance, God gave me a word for a woman, who had an abortion years ago. When God gave me the word, He didn't let me know she had an abortion in the past.

I saw a vision of her helping women who were thinking about having abortions. I saw her leading women to encounter Jesus, Whose presence is the Truth in Love that eradicates the destructive lies of the enemy. In my vision these women didn't abort their babies because they encountered Jesus through this woman.

Then, I saw the woman in heaven being greeted by

thousands of people. They were thanking her for her boldness to help their mothers choose life over death. Because of her courage to bring the truth of Jesus, these people were born and lived incredible lives.

When I told the woman this, she began to cry. She said she had a heart to do exactly what I shared, but she felt disqualified because she had an abortion years ago. After we prayed, I could see her set free from the shame and guilt that had gripped her for so long, and she was filled up with a supernatural boldness to bring good news to the poor, freedom to the broken-hearted, and set the captives free.

Like Steve, my interaction with this woman was not to condemn or disqualify her for her past. Rather, I leaned into seeing her as God sees her, and treated her as His treasure. If, as Christ's ambassadors, we truly believe that we can activate the kingdom of heaven in every situation, we should be praying for interactions like Steve had on a daily basis instead of avoiding them.

In every situation, we have a Biblical mandate to pray (Philippians 4:6). A friend of mine, who is an executive at a large tech company, recently shared a story with me about the overturning of *Roe vs. Wade*.

Shortly after the Supreme Court's decision, the Chief Equality and Inclusion Officer (CEIO) at his company sent a corporate-wide email expressing her disapproval of the decision. She invited all of the company's staff to a voluntary video call to grieve the outcome.

Upon receiving the email, my friend felt the Holy Spirit tell him he needs to attend the video call and declare Jesus as the Way, Truth and Life over the situation. For a week leading up to the call, my friend prayed "life" over the upcoming conversation. He joined the meeting remotely from his home, and with his microphone muted and camera disabled, he began to pray some more. Then, something incredible happened.

The CEIO, who had sent the email, reiterated her disapproval of the decision, and opened the meeting up for staff to do the same. A woman in her mid-thirties spoke first.

She shared that twenty years ago she became pregnant as a sixteen-year-old. With little means to support a child and at her boyfriend and family's urging, she decided to have an abortion.

As she pulled into the parking lot of a Planned Parenthood facility, she felt something inside of her say "life". She then shared on the call how she chose to have her baby boy, and how her son was now about to graduate college. She concluded her story by giving God the glory!

Then, another woman spoke up and shared her story about choosing life instead of aborting her baby. And she too gave God the glory. Then another woman did the same. And another.

The meeting, which was set up to grieve the federal de-legalization of abortion turned into a testimony session championing the goodness of God and the sanctity of life for the unborn.

I asked my friend how the CEIO responded. "Quite awkwardly," he replied.

What the enemy meant as a strategy to steal, kill and destroy, the Lord used to promote the abundant life we have in Christ. I believe the obedience of my friend to declare life over the situation created an atmosphere for the presence of God to show up. The women who boldly shared their personal testimonies glorified the Author of life in one of the most unlikely settings, and they manifested the kingdom of heaven in the tech space. Since then, that particular company has gone through a cultural transformation in which the gospel is no longer censored on its platform like it previously was, and Christians are able to reach millions of more people with the good news of Jesus.

As God's heirs and co-heirs with Christ, we are containers of the kingdom of heaven, who activate His superior reality wherever we go. Any inferior reality has to obey the superior reality of Jesus. When we do this, we prepare the atmosphere for people to encounter the goodness of God, which is the catalyst to repentance. Again, not out of compliance, but out of the peace and joy that passes all understanding when people get a glimpse into how much God loves and cares about them as His children. This is true in every situation, setting, and sphere – including the tech space.

4

HACKING HUMANS

"For we are God's handiwork, created in Christ Jesus to do good works, which God prepared in advance for us to do."
Ephesians 2:10 NIV

"Will the future be human?" That is the question Dr. Yuval Noah Harari posed in his presentation to a crowded room of the world's most influential politicians and business leaders at the 2018 World Economic Forum. It was a rhetorical question.

Dr. Harari, a professor in the Department of History at the Hebrew University of Jerusalem and best-selling author of books focusing on the history and future of humankind, went on to enlighten the audience of elites that a new superhuman species will arise within the next 200 years, replacing Homo sapiens. He predicted that a new bioengineered transhuman species will emerge that will be controlled by algorithms telling them who they are and what to do, as the coming generations learn to hack and engineer the human body through biometric data and computers powered by Artificial Intelligence (AI) and Machine Learning (ML).

The concept of a transhuman species comes from the philosophical and scientific movement "transhumanism", which advocates for the use of advanced technologies (such as the aforementioned AI and ML) to augment the human condition.[55] Transhumanists believe that technology will slow, reverse, or even eliminate the aging process, and set forth an evolutionary path in which technology will lead to an enhanced species that transcends humanity.[56]

According to Harari, we are living in an age of two revolutions, infotech and biotech. When the two intersect, we will be able to hack humans and create algorithms that know us better than we know ourselves. Harari believes this will be done through biometric sensors that translate biochemical processes in the body and brain into electronic signals a computer can store and analyze.

"You can summarize 150 years of biological research since Darwin into three words," he shared at the World Economic Forum. "Organisms are algorithms…just biochemical algorithms."

Data is now considered the most valuable commodity in the world. It is more valuable than gold and oil; and unlike both gold and oil, it is infinite. So valuable, that is has spawned an emerging ideology called "dataism", which glorifies "information flow" as having supreme value in the universe. Really though, dataism is just the idolatrous worship of Mammon wrapped up in a shiny new package.

Mammon is the spirit of greed, pertaining to money and riches. Jesus said that man cannot serve both God and Mammon. He will hate the one and love the other, or else be loyal to one and despise the other (Matthew 6:24).

God is the giver of good gifts. He is not opposed to

wealth, and He calls His children to be faithful stewards of earthly finances and material goods. In fact, the Bible says that handling earthly riches with integrity unlocks a greater privilege to handle the eternal treasure of the kingdom of heaven. When we steward finances well, we point to God's goodness and use the resources He's blessed us with to bless others, helping to lead others into an eternal relationship with the Father (Luke 16:9-11).

The gift of money and wealth is not the issue. Rather, it is the love of money and wealth that is the root of all evil (I Timothy 6:10). The moment the gift is elevated over the Giver, it perverts the gift and draws our attention away from the Giver. We will always worship what we value the most.

If data is the most valuable commodity and is pursued over or apart from God, then it becomes a god in which its worshippers draw their identity and self-worth. With that in mind, take a look at the scenario Harari described could play out in the future:

Humans don't really know ourselves. When I was 21, I realized I was gay. I didn't know myself—living many years in denial…

Now imagine the situation in 10-20 years an algorithm that can tell any teenager where he or she is on the gay/straight spectrum, and even how malleable this position is. The algorithm tracks your eye movements, blood pressure, and brain activity, and tells you who you are…

Maybe you find yourself at some boring birthday party from someone in your class at school, and one of your friends has a wonderful idea that "I just heard of this new algorithm that tells you your sexual orientation." And wouldn't it be fun if everyone takes turns on this algorithm while everyone else watches and comments. What would you do? Would you just walk away?

And even if you walk away, hiding from your classmates and yourself, you will not be able to hide from Amazon, Alibaba and the secret police. As you surf the internet, watch videos and your social feed, the algorithms will be monitoring your blood pressure and brain activity... They will know and could tell Coca-Cola, "Don't use the ad with the shirtless girl, but with the shirtless guy." This info will be worth billions… The algorithm can predict my desires, manipulate my emotions and even take decisions on my behalf.[57]

The real question Harari poses is not *if* a transhuman biotech species will replace Homo sapiens within the next 200 years, or if it's ethically right or wrong to lead humans down the path. The real question and the perceived problem to solve in his mind is: who controls the data when it happens, and will they create a new form of tyranny through digital dictatorships?

Harari continues:

But control of data, might enable human elites to do something more radical than digital dictatorships. By hacking organisms, elites may gain the power to re-engineer the future of life itself. Because once you can hack something, you can usually re-engineer it. If we succeed, it will be the greatest revolution of humanity and biology since the beginning of life four billion years ago.

For four billion years nothing fundamental changed in the basic rules in the game of life. All of life was subject to the laws of natural selection and organic biochemistry.

But this is now about to change. Science is replacing evolution by natural selection with evolution of intelligent design. Not design from some god above the clouds, but our intelligent design in the cloud. IBM and Microsoft, these are the new driving forces of evolution.

The ownership of data is so important. If we don't regulate the control of data, we could see a tiny elite come to control the future of human society.

Does my data belong to the corporation, government, or human collective? At present, big corporations are holding much of the data…

I think the world is divided into a very small group of people who know what's at stake and the vast majority of ordinary people, politicians and business people who don't know what's at stake.

The usual "big tech" understand what's at stake. The Chinese government knows what's at stake. We are 5-10 years away from having the technology. It's a race to the button. No country wants to fall behind.[58]

Do you see the evolution paradigm shift in what Harari proposes is happening? The idea of natural selection has given way to intelligent design. Not intelligent design from the Creator of the universe, but intelligent design birthed from the minds of humans, presenting a paradox in which the human mind is devising its own demise through the perceived notion of innovating humanity forward. The race to the button, as Harari suggests, is really a race to the bottom.

Our origin of existence reveals our identity. If we are created by God, as His children, our identity is rooted in purpose as a son or daughter of our Father. But, if our origin of existence is the result of an accident billions of years ago, our identity is what we decide in the perpetual journey of trying to fix and perfect ourselves. In the latter explanation, we are on a path of perfecting ourselves into extinction.

The common thread in the lie of evolution is the enemy's desire to steal, kill and destroy humanity. We see it in the dehumanization of a people-group based on ethnicity. We see it in society's acceptance and celebration of abortion. And now we risk perpetuating the next iteration of the lie through the potential subjugation of humans through the algorithmic whims of artificial intelligence (AI).

AI is the science of making computers that think like humans. It does this through algorithms that make predictions or classifications based on analyzing large amounts of data.

There are two types of artificial intelligence: strong and weak AI. Strong AI consists of Artificial General Intelligence (AGI) and Artificial Super Intelligence (ASI). As described by IBM, AGI is "a theoretical form of AI where a machine would have an intelligence equaled to humans; it would have a self-aware consciousness that has the ability to solve problems, learn, and plan for the future."[59] AGI has no practical examples in use today, but in theory, it would "surpass the intelligence and ability of the human brain."[60]

This is where the concept of the moment of singularity comes into play. Singularity refers to the point in time when AI surpasses the brain power of humans, evolves on its own, and exceeds human control. Essentially, humans become slaves to the computers they've built.

But weak (or narrow) AI, which is trained to perform specific tasks, is very much in use today, and has become a part of our everyday lives. Apple's Siri and Amazon's Alexa fall into this category.

In November of 2022, the San Francisco-based tech company OpenAI launched ChatGPT – the most advanced narrow artificial intelligence chatbot ever released to the general public. A chatbot is a software application designed to simulate conversations with humans online.[61] Log into your mobile or television service provider account online, and you're sure to be greeted by chatbot, posing as a human.

ChatGPT is a general language processing model that is trained on large libraries of spoken human language and text. Its AI is so sophisticated that it goes beyond mimicking general human conversation. Ask it to write or debug a computer program, and it will do so quite effectively in less than three seconds. Ask it to write a college essay on the impact of Christianity on Western culture in the 1800s, and it will push out a paper in no time that is indistinguishable from the work of an above-average college student.

Mind you, this is also based on learning from human speech. Once it uses real-world data (probably within the next year), the quality of its output could be far superior to what most humans would produce. This could be the key that unlocks the door to AGI or ASI.

AI is a great tool to automate tasks such as Siri telling you the daily weather forecast or Alexa dimming the lights in your home. But to automate creative human expression, ingenuity and intuition is to deprive humanity of the uniqueness that

God breathed in each individual. And to replace human intuition in the decision-making process with AI is a dangerous road to travel.

In 1976, the American Philosopher Judith Thompson wrote an article that popularized a thought experiment in human ethics and psychology called the "trolley problem".[62] The experiment posed a scenario in which a runaway trolley car is on course to hit a group of people standing on the track. The driver has access to a switch that would divert the trolley to another track, on which one person stands. The driver must decide whether he should do nothing and risk killing the five people on the current track or shift the car to the other track and kill the one person. The idea is far-fetched, but the purpose of the experiment is to reveal to what extent someone will sacrifice the one for the good of the many.

A few years ago, a friend of mine, who works on the Google team that builds the AI for self-driving cars, shared with me how her team faces the 2.0 version of the trolley problem. She described how her team struggles with the dilemma of building AI that will replace the human decision-making process in a situation where a potentially fatal collision appears unavoidable. For example, in a potential collision does the software give preference to the people inside or outside of the car? The question that she constantly asks herself is: just because we *can* build the technology, *should* we?

As AI continues down the path toward AGI, it still won't be able to account for the unpredictable workings of the human brain and ingenuity of the human mind; nor will it be able to assign meaning to the information that it processes.

Computers are intricately-designed digital machines based on logic, reproducibility, predictability, and mathematics. They work by going step by step through a list of instructions encoded in a memory bank.[63]

The human brain, on the other hand, is a seemingly random entanglement of billions of neurons that behave unpredictably.[64] And created within the human brain is the human mind, which assigns meaning and nuance to information. It instinctively creates solutions in conceivably impossible situations; and unconsciously calculates the slightest of possibilities in the blink of an eye.

In 2012, a 22-year-old woman in Virginia lifted a car off her father when it toppled from a jack. A few years earlier, a man did the same for a trapped cyclist in Tucson, Arizona. For context, the world deadlift record is a little over 1,100 pounds, and a car weighs about 3,000 pounds.[65]

Logic would say there is no way one person has the strength to pick up a car and rescue a trapped individual. Analyzing data from thousands of similar situations, AI would conclude that a human lifting the car by themselves is not a viable solution and should not be included in the data set that AI would use to automate the decision-making process. And yet, the heroes in the aforementioned examples sprang into action, making seemingly illogical and improbable split-second decisions that saved lives.

Typically, the body tends to use the least amount of energy to perform an action. Researchers estimate that the average person exerts 60 percent of muscle capacity during high intensity exercise, leaving 40 percent in energy reserve.[66]

The brain holds back energy to keep the body safe. At 100 percent capacity, an individual could tear muscles, break bones, or die from exhaustion.

But in life-or-death situations, the brain can deploy hysterical strength, bypassing its self-imposed limits to allow 100 percent energy use.[67] The human brain taps into an unused reservoir of strength and decision-making to find a solution to an otherwise impossible situation.

In Google's Trolley Problem 2.0, there is no amount of AI programming that can account for human will and the unpredictable genius and creativity of the human mind. It cannot bypass the limits that have been imposed on it by its developers.

We cannot take the keys out of human hands to make instinctive decisions in times of crisis. In the same way a human finds a way to lift a car off an individual, a human also has the potential to find an inconceivable solution to the trolley problem so that no lives are lost.

Science and technology must not remove the instinctual, seemingly illogical human decision-making process from our society. If we do, then we risk fulfilling Harari's doomsday prediction of the end of the human species.

I believe artificial intelligence, as powerful as it is (and is becoming), is an inferior technology. No matter how sophisticated technologists build it, AI is still the product of human input and training.

The danger of AI is hidden in its very name. AI is an artificial alternative to the ingenuity, creativity and reasoning embedded in our DNA by the Creator Who made us in His image.

In July 2022, OpenAI CEO Sam Altman tweeted that AGI is probably necessary for humanity to survive because "our problems seem too big for us to solve without better tools." He said that the downside of AGI could mean that it's lights out for all of us.[68]

Altman is correct to say that our problems are too big for us to solve without better tools. His statement is akin to the Ancient Greeks building the statue to the unknown God.

It took the Apostle Paul showing up to reveal the truth that Jesus is the unknown solution they were seeking, in Whom we live and move and have our being. And it will take Kingdom-minded believers to show up in the tech space that create the tools that point to Jesus as the solution to the problems that are too big for humans to solve apart from God.

5

WHERE WAS THE CHURCH?

"You are the light of the world. A city that is set on a hill cannot be hidden. Nor do they light a lamp and put it under a basket, but on a lampstand, and it gives light to all who are in the house. Let your light so shine before men, that they may see your good works and glorify your Father in heaven."
Matthew 5:14-16 NKJV

Jesus calls His followers the light of the world, who shine before men so that they may see their good works and glorify our heavenly Father. Light always dispels darkness, but it must be present in order to do so.

Which begs the question: where was the church while the lie of evolution spread its destructive tentacles into every area of society over the last 150 years? Where was the light-producing good work in science and technology that glorified our Creator, so that all would taste and see His goodness?

There are a number of differing perspectives among theologians and church leaders on the church's absence in influential spheres of society over the last 150 years. This topic of conversation often shifts toward eschatology, mostly around premillennialism and postmillennialism

I'm less concerned about igniting another theological debate on the end times, and I'm more concerned about the current state of the church's absence in the influential sphere of science and technology. As I mentioned earlier, the future of work is in tech. In Silicon Valley, the mecca of the tech space, it is estimated that over 80 percent of the workforce identifies as either atheist or agnostic.

My perspective on eschatology is simple: go and share the love of Christ in word and deed to everyone, everywhere. Jesus said the end will come when the gospel is preached all over the world, demonstrating the reality of God to every nation (Matthew 24:14).

However you want to perceive that verse, one thing is certain: the testimony of Jesus will be proclaimed to everyone. It is an encounter with His love that leads people to a revelation of their origin of design, which is an eternal relationship with our loving Father. And Christians get to be His hands and feet to usher in that revelation.

Jesus told the disciples it is not for you to know the times or seasons of the last days. Instead, He charged them to go in boldness with the power of the Holy Spirit and bring the gospel to all the ends of the earth (Acts 1:7). Keeping the testimony of Jesus the main thing, we should all have a sense of urgency to lead people to an encounter with His love, engaging every sphere of society.

There were (and still are) Christians in the sphere of science and technology who have made a significant impact on the world since Maxwell. But many influential Christians in science and technology, post-Maxwell, have accepted the reconciliation of evolution and Christianity, interweaving the two in a sordid explanation of our origin story.

I believe species do adapt over time, as preexisting genetic information is changed or lost through sexual reproduction, producing small changes within a species. This is often referred to as microevolution.[69]

Such a change might occur because a population of the *same* species carrying a different gene migrated to a new region and bred with the indigenous population to produce offspring that would then carry the same gene.[70] This would make sense with Darwin's finches on the Galapagos islands.

But macroevolution, the idea that we are the random result of billions of years of interspecies transition, in which new genetic information is added over time from species to species, does not add up. We are not the descendants of apes.

Launched in 1990, The Human Genome Project (HGP) was a 13-year research initiative to discover all of the 20,000-25,000 human genes, as well as determine the complete sequence of the 3 billion DNA subunits in the human genome.[71] The assumption among the evolutionists was the project would further validate evolution as the unifying principle of human origin and biology. Their hope was to find the gene that linked primate to human that proved interspecies evolution.

It didn't go as planned.

As the researchers studied the human genome, they found that human DNA was so stable that interspecies transition was not possible. The project revealed that similar organs between species are not created from the same genetic code.[72]

There was no missing link. Yet, the theory of interspecies

evolution carries on as the widely-accepted explanation for humankind's origin of existence.

When an idea is accepted and standardized as truth, it becomes the starting point for all exploration. In the area of science, archeological findings and observations of natural occurrences are no longer meant to question the validity of evolution. Rather, they serve to validate its perceived and accepted truth, and allow people to perpetuate a cycle of inference based on confirmation bias that, over time, shifts to unconscious bias.

Inference is the basis of the standard view of origin in the scientific community, but it's really just a clinical way of describing a leap of faith - the very thing evolutionists accuse creationists of doing. What one generation tolerates as truth, the next generation will accept, and the next will adopt and standardize.

In the film *Nacho Libre,* the main character "Nacho Libre" tells his assistant he is concerned for his salvation and he needs to be baptized. To which his assistant responds he only believes in science. Nacho Libre then fills up a bowl with water, and surprise-baptizes his assistant by sneaking up behind him and forcing his head into the bowl of water.

It's hilarious! And if you haven't seen the movie; at least go on YouTube and watch the scene. It's 48 seconds of ridiculous comedy!

But it also represents the perceived and accepted chasm that exists between Christianity and science. And one thing is for certain: since Maxwell, Christianity and science have veered in opposite, seemingly irreconcilable directions.

At Bethel Church, we have a core value of creating legacy in which one generation's ceiling is the next generation's floor. I believe the Body of Christ did not take what Maxwell set in motion to move humanity heavenward in the sphere of science and technology. Instead, the Church distanced itself from science as Darwin's theory of evolution took root and shaped society's belief of origin.

Around the same time that Maxwell and Darwin were publishing their theories in the second half of the 19th century, an Irish minister named John Nelson Darby, a member of the Plymouth Brethren in England, traveled across Western Europe and the United States preaching dispensational premillennialism eschatology.

Dispensational premillennialism is the belief that history can be divided into seven dispensations, or ages. In the current age (the age of the church), the world will continue to get worse and worse until Jesus raptures his followers. The rapture is followed by a great tribulation in which an antichrist will have reign over the people left behind and the world will fall into an absolute evil state.

After the tribulation, Jesus will return to earth to take up the believers who received Him during the tribulation, and He will judge the earth, sending the antichrist and his followers to eternal damnation in hell. After judgment day, Jesus will set up a millennial reign of peace on earth over His followers.

Prior to Darby, Christians in the United States largely held a postmillennial view that the world would continue to get better and better as all the nations heard the good news of Jesus and accepted Him as their Lord and Savior. They believed that after receiving salvation, people would walk in their identities as God's children and bring heaven on earth, preparing a place for Jesus to set up His millennial reign of peace. Charles Finney and the Second Great Awakening were influential for spreading postmillennial eschatology, and Christians were encouraged to engage and elevate all areas of society to magnify the goodness of God.

But premillennialism started to gain traction. And devastating world events would seem to validate Darby's theology, who traveled across the U.S. in the 1860s and shared his message at the same time as the Civil War. The war was and still is the bloodiest war fought on U.S. soil, in some cases, pitting brother against brother and neighbor against neighbor. As the country buried its dead, it certainly didn't feel like the world was getting better. The country seemed to be spiraling toward total ruin.

In 1889, a flood devastated the town of Johnstown, PA, killing over 2,200 people.[73] In 1900, a Category 4 hurricane ripped through Galveston, TX killing an estimated 6,000-8,000 people in what is still the deadliest natural disaster in U.S. history.[74] In 1906, a major earthquake devastated San Francisco, CA killing an estimated 3,000 people and destroying 80 percent of the city.[75]

Then, in 1914, World War I broke out, and it was official: the world was going to hell in a hand-basket. It seemed Darby's premillennialism was true, and Christ's return to rapture His followers was imminent since the world was on the verge of total despair.

It was of little importance in the minds of many premillennialists of the day to influence and move forward areas of society that would soon be of no consequence. Science and its rising narrative of an anti-creation evolution was the sophisticated, overt weapon in the devil's tool belt to destroy society, even though Maxwell had just ushered in a profound epoch in science and technology based on Holy Spirit-led innovation. The church left the science lab, so to speak.

During this time period, there were legendary evangelists, such as Smith Wigglesworth, Maria Woodworth-Etter, William J. Seymour, and John G. Lake, who led hundreds of thousands of people to the Lord. And in the science and technology sphere, there was Dr. George Washington Carver.

A former slave, Carver was the first Black student at Iowa State University in 1891; and he later became the first Black professor at his alma mater.[76] He was an agricultural genius who discovered over 300 uses for the peanut, and he revolutionized the way farmers prepare and nurture soil for crops.[77]

In 1921, Carver spoke to the U.S. House Ways and Means Committee on the peanut industry, which his discoveries largely created.[78] The chairman was so blown away with Carver's ingenuity, he asked him how he knew so much about the peanut. Carver said that the Bible had led him to his discoveries. "Does the Bible tell about peanuts?" the chairman followed-up. "No sir," Carver replied. "But it tells about the God who made the peanut. I asked Him to show me what to do with the peanut, and He did."[79]

But outside of Dr. Carver, the church didn't take Maxwell's baton, and it neglected the science and technology community. This absence gave way for the enemy to pull the strings in the highly influential space, pointing to a false origin of existence. So much so, that much of the church today has raised the white flag, feeding the narrative that Christianity and the tech space are in perpetual opposition with each other.

THE GOD OF TECH

But all hope is not lost. God is calling up a new generation of Maxwells, who will partner with Him to manifest His creativity from the unseen heavenly realm into the physical world to reveal His goodness through science and technology.

I believe we are nearing the end of one epoch in science started by Maxwell, and entering into a new epoch of technological discovery and innovation that will point back to God as our Creator and loving Father. It will be as revolutionary as what Maxwell set in motion over 150 years ago, and it will be incomprehensible to man apart from God.

The greatest form of intelligence in this new season will come directly from faith in God, and it will be this faith that uncovers the manifestation and evidence of things not yet seen. It is the promise of a hopeful future in which we will eradicate the lies of the deceiver, and replace it with the truth of our Redeemer.

The very nature of the next epoch in science will reveal the brilliance of our Creator and His relationship with creation. And, it will be fully actualized by Christ-followers receiving spiritual downloads from God to move humanity heavenward.

6

THE NEXT EPOCH

"If you think you understand quantum mechanics, you don't understand quantum mechanics." - Richard Feynman

On May 6, 1981, over 50 scientists gathered for the Physics of Computation Conference. Co-hosted by IBM and MIT at MIT's Endicott House in Dedham, Massachusetts, the three-day event served as a pivotal moment in the acceleration of quantum physics and computing.

Introduced around the turn of the 20th century by Max Planck, quantum physics (or quantum mechanics) describes the smallest parts of the world - atoms and subatomic particles - and how they affect our universe. It is based on the idea that the universe, at its core, is composed of invisible information that explains its existence, marked by scientific phenomena that is unfathomable to the human mind.

Prior to the conference at Endicott, quantum physics wasn't considered much more than a sci-fi fantasy approach to explain the universe, and its public perception often fell closer to the category of new age mysticism than empirical science. In 1981, you weren't going to find any job openings for quantum physicists in the newspaper classifieds, because they just didn't exist.

The conference attendees were discoverers at heart, who sought to rationalize and harness the unexplainable components of quantum mechanics. They were rogue pioneers in the world of quantum, creating a new frontier as they pursued it, who, up until the conference, had little exposure to each other's theories and work.

At the time, Apple and IBM personal computers were starting to pop up in homes, schools and libraries. And, the tech space was snowballing toward a tipping point of innovation and advancement in the world of classical computing that would usher in the digital age of mainstream internet, laptops, Wi-Fi and cell phones. Society was on the cusp of an info tech revolution, and nothing was going to slow it down—certainly not an illogical and unexplainable science like quantum physics.

At the conference, California Institute of Technology professor and Nobel laureate, Richard Feynman, ignited a flame among the Endicott scientists when he proposed the idea of a quantum computer. Remember Feynman? He is the renowned physicist who pointed to Maxwell's equations as the single most important scientific discovery of the 19th century.

"Nature isn't classical," Feynman shared at the conference. "And if you want to make a simulation of nature, you'd better make it quantum mechanical, and by golly it's a wonderful problem, because it doesn't look so easy."[80]

Building on top of this one statement, Feynman introduced the idea of a quantum computer, which set into motion a shared goal among the attendees to achieve it.

Feynman provided the rally cry, perhaps unintentionally, that bonded the Endicott scientists as a close-knit community of quantum innovators.[81]

So what is quantum computing? And how is it different from the computers you and I use every day?

Our current computers are based on classical computing, using binary digits (or bits). Bits are streams of electrical or optical pulses represented by a "1" or a "0". Everything we do on classical computers, from sending emails to watching videos, is basically made up of long strings of bits based on either/or algebraic logic.[82]

Quantum computers do not operate on bits. Instead, they use qubits, which are typically subatomic particles, like electrons or photons. Whereas a classical bit can either be 0 or 1, a qubit can represent the values 0 and 1, or some combination of both at the same time.

The combination of qubits creates an exponential number of states, of which a quantum algorithm can then compute all possible inputs at the same time. This allows for an exponentially faster, more-optimized way to store, transport, and compute data than classical computing. The data that would take today's fastest classical supercomputers years to process, will take a quantum computer seconds or minutes.

If classical computing is confined to the limitations of "either/or" logic and calculations, perhaps, as Feynman proposed to the scientists at the Endicott house, the ability to build a computer that simulates nature could tap into the vast mysteries of the universe beyond logic.

Qubits behave in strange ways that physicists can't fully explain. And two quantum properties in particular have left physicists scratching their heads for years.

The first is called superposition. In this quantum phenomenon, a subatomic particle (i.e. an electron) exists in two states at once, as both a wave and a particle, through a quantum feature called spin. In a magnetic field, the electron may exist in two possible spin states—spin up and down.

Scientists create qubits by finding a spot in a subatomic particle where they can access and control the quantum spin, using lasers, microwave beams, and magnets. A quantum computer operating with several qubits in superposition can compute a large number of potential outcomes simultaneously. Only when the qubit (electron) is measured or observed does it collapse from wave function into a particle, and the final calculation emerges as either a 1 or 0.

Think about it like spinning a coin. During the spin, the coin is both heads and tails. It's not until someone stops and observes the coin that it is identified as heads or tails up. We will discuss the collapse of a subatomic particle in further detail shortly.

When two separate qubits are in superposition they can be linked together in quantum entanglement. With entanglement, two separate qubits - their positions, speeds, and spins - become connected as a single quantum state. Meaning, an action performed on one instantly affects the other in a predictable way, even if they are miles apart from each other.

Information is transported or, dare I say, teleported instantaneously from one qubit to another, because the transport is not a matter of transferring through space and time (or spacetime as Einstein called it).[83] Rather, it's a matter of the qubits being connected and correlated with each other. Einstein called this quantum mechanics' "spooky action from a distance," because it suggests that information can travel faster than the speed of light, defying the physics of spacetime.

Entanglement is the key to quantum computing. In a classical computer, doubling the number of bits doubles the processing power. In quantum computers, adding extra entangled qubits increases the machine's processing power exponentially.[84]

But the quantum state of qubits in superposition and entanglement is extremely sensitive. The smallest disturbance or "noise", such as a vibration or a slight change in temperature, can cause the quantum state to disappear. This is called decoherence.

Scientists and researchers do their best to reduce noise by housing qubits in supercooled fridges at temperatures colder than deep space.[85] Still, qubits are extremely error-prone, and it would take thousands of standard qubits to create a highly-reliable quantum computer.

In the 40 years since the Physics of Computation Conference at Endicott, the field of quantum computing has progressed at an accelerated rate compared to the century prior to it. And futurists believe the actualization of quantum computers will lead to finding solutions for seemingly unsolvable problems, like finding cures for incurable diseases and developing unhackable cyber security.

In the case of finding cures for previously incurable diseases, quantum computing provides chemists a much faster and more complex simulation of molecules than even today's fastest super computers, and it increases the potential of discovering new molecules. With quantum computing, researchers could improve the speed of disease diagnosis and treatment, discover new drugs, and build treatments customized to a person's specific molecule discrepancy in a disease like cancer.[86]

As for building unhackable cyber security, the very nature of quantum physics presents a superior form of cryptography. Cryptography is the science of creating secret communication techniques to transmit secure information from a sender to a receiver.

In quantum cryptography, it's seemingly impossible for a hacker to steal information sent via an encoded key using entangled qubits. Based on the behavior of entangled particles, if someone tries to intercept the quantum key, the key will immediately change – making the interference obvious to the sender. Detecting the change, the sender will throw the key out and create a new one.[87]

In 2022, IBM achieved an important milestone when it built a 433-qubit quantum computer, up from the 127-qubit computer it built the year prior. And the company plans to build a 4,000 qubit quantum computer by 2025.[88]

The global quantum computing market is projected to reach $8.6 billion in revenue (and more than $16 billion in investments) by 2027.[89] Leading tech companies like Google, IBM, and Microsoft are hiring the top quantum physicists in the world, spending hundreds of millions of dollars to be the first company that builds a working, commercialized quantum computer. China and the United States have invested billions of dollars respectively to do the same. In May 2022, the White House issued a national security memo to advance quantum technologies. The global powers are in a race to achieve quantum supremacy.

The fruit of the conference at Endicott was a power group

of innovators sharing their ideas on quantum physics and providing a quantum computing moonshot that would inspire others outside of the conference to build upon their ideas, including Peter Shor. In 1994, Shor, who was an applied mathematician at Bell Labs, published his namesake algorithm that demonstrated quantum computers could simulate physics and factor really large numbers into their primes exponentially faster than classical computing. This, like the conference at Endicott, proved to be an anchor point in the field of quantum computing.

Like Feynman, Shor understood that the world of quantum was non-intuitive and often unexplainable. In a culture built on classical computing's true/false logic, those outside the quantum computing world were still quick to dismiss something that made absolutely no sense. In response to critics, Shor wrote the following poem:

THIS IS NO CLOCKWORK UNIVERSE[90]

If the eternal dance of molecules
Is too entangled for us mortal fools
To follow, on what grounds should we complain?
Who promised us that Nature's arcane rules
Would make sense to a merely human brain?

Perhaps there is something more to discover with quantum mechanics and computing that goes beyond natural comprehension, as Shor suggested in the last line of his poem and Feynman shared at the Physics of Computation Conference. Maybe the peculiar, unfathomable, non-intuitive invisible workings of the quantum world cannot be fully discerned in the flesh alone, but from spirit to spirit through the mind of Christ as the Apostle Paul describes in 1 Corinthians 2:12-16 (NKJV):

> Now we have received, not the spirit of the world, but the Spirit who is from God, that we might know the things that have been freely given to us by God. These things we also speak, not in words which man's wisdom teaches but which the Holy Spirit teaches, comparing spiritual things with spiritual. But the natural man does not receive the things of the Spirit of God, for they are foolishness to him; nor can he know them, because they are spiritually discerned. But he who is spiritual judges all things, yet he himself is rightly judged by no one. For "who has known the mind of the LORD that he may instruct Him?" But we have the mind of Christ.

Perhaps the very nature of quantum is a compass pointing back to its Creator, heralded by the subatomic particles of the universe crying out that Jesus is King. And, perhaps the unexplainable phenomena of superposition and entanglement are signs and wonders from a superior realm.

II.

Let's jump into the quantum properties Feynman and Shor referenced when they suggested the quantum world isn't fully comprehensible to the human mind. It doesn't sit well with the scientific community to identify occurrences as phenomena. To the scientist, anything that can be observed or experienced must be explained through empirical evidence or "logical" inference.

As I mentioned before, the concept of phenomena is the human mind's attempt to rationalize signs and wonders from God. Discovering the origin of these phenomena is a key that unlocks a revival in which science reveals Him as our Creator and loving Father who longs for relationship with all of His children.

Today, I believe we are on the verge of the next epoch of tech innovation that will be ushered in by quantum computing and revealing its phenomena as signs and wonders from heaven. At its premise, quantum physics points to a multi-dimensional nature in which physical objects are permanently connected in an underlying reality.

Quantum computing represents a more "true-to-nature" method of sending and receiving data than classical computing, and experts believe we are anywhere from five years to decades away from quantum computing becoming mainstream. In 2019, scientists at the University of Bristol and the Technical University of Denmark achieved quantum teleportation of data between two computer chips (qubits) for the first time.[91]

And right now, the leading tech companies in the world are in a race to reimagine the computer using quantum mechanics, employing the leading quantum physicists, who are splitting the atom into smaller subatomic particles. What they are finding when they further dissect the atom into smaller particles is that these particles move and function in an inexplicable way. So much so, that many scientists have determined there must be a guiding force in another universe directing their movement.

A friend of mine who works in R&D at one of the leading

tech companies explained it to me this way:

> The closer we look at physics and particles, the more we
> realize we don't really understand what 'matter' even is,
> and the only way we can accurately model or represent
> particle physics is by assuming infinitive worlds or realities.
> The deeper we go, the stranger and more bizarre the
> theories must become in order to explain existence.

It's as though the stones are crying out that Jesus is king.
And, the door is opening in the hearts of scientists who are
hungry and willing to find the source.

One of Stephen Hawking's last papers before his death in
2018 was on this idea that there were multiple universes put
into motion billions of years ago as a result of the Big Bang.
He suggested that these other universes interact with and
affect our universe to create phenomena we can't fully
explain. It's what Hawking and other scientists refer to as
multiverse theory, or many worlds interpretation, and it's
gained a lot of steam over the last 30 years because it's the
only "logical" scientific explanation for the quantum
phenomena of superposition and entanglement.

But, is it more logical to believe that an accidental event
billions of years ago set our entire existence into motion than
it is to believe that God created the heavens and the earth?
The question still remains: From where did the big bang
moment of existence originate?"

Science and tech innovation appear to be pointing towards
an advanced state of operating in both the natural world and
heavenly realm simultaneously. Think about it: a qubit in
superposition can be in two states simultaneously–much like

believers, who are here on earth, but also simultaneously seated in heavenly places (Ephesians 2:6).

In entanglement, two qubits become exactly correlated with each other. A measurement of one will immediately determine the measurement of the other, regardless of distance. Information can be transferred instantly, because it's not a matter of being transported through spacetime. It's a matter of connection.

As children of God, we have the mind of Christ. We don't just know of Him; we know Him and are "entangled" as one with Him. As He is in the world, so are we (1 John 4:17).

It's a beautiful microcosm of God's desire for communion relationship with His children. I believe that fully actualizing its potential will lead us to reveal Emmanuel, Christ with us, as we pull solutions from the unseen realm into our natural world to help people. These solutions will serve as building blocks to magnify His goodness.

Now let's dive a little deeper into superposition, for a moment, and the collapsing of a wave function into a particle. For years, scientists have been trying to wrap their heads around the results of the double-slit experiment. The experiment consists of shooting subatomic particles (i.e. electrons) from a ray gun one at a time at a wall that has two vertical slits in it right next to each other. Behind the wall is another wall to catch the particles that travel through the slits.

The results are peculiar, to say the least. Instead of forming two straight lines on the back wall to reflect the pattern of the particles passing through the slits, as one would assume, the particles don't behave like particles at all. They behave like waves, spreading out into semi-circular ripples and passing through the two slits.

When the waves pass through the two slits, two sets of ripples (one per slit) form and then intersect with each other, creating a horizontal wave pattern on the back wall. Scientists rationalize that each particle must exist in two states at once—both as a "wave potential," allowing it to pass through both slits, and a physical particle, allowing it to interfere with itself creating a horizontal particle pattern on the back wall.

Now, here's where it gets really wild. Scientists will place a measuring device or detector near the slits to observe which slit the electron passes through. When they shoot the electrons through the slits being measured by the detector, the electrons stop behaving like waves, and only behave like tiny particles, creating a pattern of two vertical lines on the back wall, as one would originally assume. The electrons collapse from wave to physical particle only when observed by the detector.

All matter, including humans, are made up of billions of subatomic particles bound together, which, based on the double-slit experiment, only exist as matter once they are observed. The material that makes up our physical existence must first be observed in order to collapse from a wave potential into a physical state. Therefore, it stands to reason, there must be an Observer who has first thought about and seen in His mind all creation, including people.

The Observer is conscious of the electron; and, subsequently the electron is conscious of the Observer. The consciousness must first exist with the Observer, and then be transferred to the "observed" before it can become aware of what it is.

Let's say I asked you to draw on paper the first thing that comes to your mind. Perhaps an image of a circle popped into your head, and so you drew a circle. The circle first had to be a thought in your mind. Before it was a thought in your mind, the image could have been anything within the vast mental database of your mind.

You could have chosen anything, but you chose a circle. And not just a circle. Perhaps, you chose a circle with a specific color and size. Then, that circle had to be observed by your mind's eye. And then it had to be acted upon through your handiwork to go from a wave of potential in your mind to a physical manifestation in the natural world for everyone to see and experience.

When God created humans, He said, "Let us make man in Our image, according to our likeness" (Genesis 1:26). God thought about you, observed a picture of you in His imagination and spoke that picture into existence. He knew you and gave you purpose before He formed you in your mother's womb (Jeremiah 1:5). And, He chose you to be His very own, joining you to Himself before He laid the foundation of the universe (Ephesians 1:4). He could have chosen anything to imagine, but He chose to imagine you!

You are God's craftsmanship (Ephesians 2:10) and the apple of His eye (Psalms 17:8). You are the impossible dream manifested into the physical realm from a beautiful picture imagined by the Creator of the universe. And you, being made in His image, are bound and entangled with Him so that He resides in you and you in Him to do the incredible things He planned for you from the beginning of time.

Separation from the Creator is a matter of listening to the wrong voice, urging you to question what God says about you and telling you that your identity is rooted in some random accidental occurrence. In quantum speak, the belief in the lies of the deceiver is the noise that leads to the decoherence of creation's entanglement with its Creator.

If the best way to build a quantum computer is to simulate physics or nature, then it's only natural to begin with the Creator who imagined and spoke the worlds into existence. To recognize this origin is the key to unlocking the full potential of quantum physics and computing. To what glorious extent, I'm not totally sure. But I sense that a new science is on the horizon that will make our current technologies in areas such as communication and transportation look prehistoric.

III.

Sometimes when I share on the topic of quantum computing and its potential, I have someone tell me that humans will be able to teleport in the future. I don't know if that will be the case, but I do believe it's possible. In fact, we have record of it in the Bible.

After Jesus rose from the grave, He appeared to the disciples, who had locked themselves together in a room for fear they too would be executed. When He appeared to them, He showed the disciples the wounds on his hands and sides to prove that He was in the flesh and not a ghost (Luke 24:36-40).

One of the disciples in the room was Philip. Remember, Philip was the one Jesus asked how they would feed the five thousand. The question was an invitation to Philip and the other disciples to think with the mind of Christ, and manifest a Divine solution from the invisible realm to solve a problem in the physical world. Jesus taught and activated His followers to manifest the superior reality of the kingdom of heaven on earth.

After Jesus's resurrection and ascension to heaven, we find in Acts 8:26-40 (NKJV) another story of Philip in which he yields in surrender to the voice of God, and heaven is deposited on earth. He too, like Jesus, teleports from one place to another, breaking through the boundaries of spacetime.

Now an angel of the Lord spoke to Philip, saying, "Arise and go toward the south along the road which goes down from Jerusalem to Gaza." This is desert.

So he arose and went. And behold, a man of Ethiopia, a eunuch of great authority under Candace the queen of the Ethiopians, who had charge of all her treasury, and had come to Jerusalem to worship, was returning. And sitting in his chariot, he was reading Isaiah the prophet.

Then the Spirit said to Philip, "Go near and overtake this chariot." So Philip ran to him, and heard him reading the prophet Isaiah, and said, "Do you understand what you are reading?"

And he said, "How can I, unless someone guides me?" And he asked Philip to come up and sit with him. The place in the Scripture which he read was this:

"He was led as a sheep to the slaughter; And as a lamb before its shearer is silent, So He opened not His mouth. In His humiliation His justice was taken away, And who will declare His generation? For His life is taken from the earth."

So the eunuch answered Philip and said, "I ask you, of whom does the prophet say this, of himself or of some other man?" Then Philip opened his mouth, and beginning at this Scripture, preached Jesus to him. Now as they went down the road, they came to some water. And the eunuch said, "See, here is water. What hinders me from being baptized?"

Then Philip said, "If you believe with all your heart, you may." And he answered and said, "I believe that Jesus Christ is the Son of God."

So he commanded the chariot to stand still. And both Philip and the eunuch went down into the water, and he baptized him. Now when they came up out of the water, the Spirit of the Lord caught Philip away, so that the eunuch saw him no more; and he went on his way rejoicing. But Philip was found at Azotus. And passing through, he preached in all the cities till he came to Caesarea.

Historians believe the eunuch in this story, upon his conversion and baptism, took the gospel back to Ethiopia and started the first church there.

Philip's first-hand experiences with the miracles of Jesus were more than individual moments of wonder in history; they became the foundation of the disciple's faith in the superior reality of the Father. After His resurrection, Jesus told the disciples, "As the Father has sent me, I am also sending you." Then He breathed on them, and they received the Holy Spirit (John 20:21-22).

Through relationship and experience with Jesus, Philip became a container of heaven. So much so that the natural reality of space and time had to yield to the voice of its Creator, allowing Philip's instantaneous teleportation. All

Philip had to do was listen to what God was saying, trust His voice, and do what He asked him to do. That is a very natural thing when you are aware that the Holy Spirit resides inside of you, entangled as one, and you become intimately in tune with His voice.

So, when individuals ask me if quantum mechanics will open up a way for humans to teleport in the future, my response to them is: why would you want to teleport, anyway?

And therein lies the fundamental question to all technology. It's more about the "why" than the "how." If the answer to that question is focused on humanity's capacity to achieve whatever we put our minds to, then I suggest we are not ready for this advancement in technology.

Innovation's true intent is to move humanity heavenward. Therefore, our "why" should always align with God's "why."

At the temple in Nazareth, Jesus was handed the scroll of the prophet Isaiah, which foretold of a Savior who would bring hope to the poor, freedom to the brokenhearted, new eyes for the blind to see, and to proclaim liberty to the captives and set them free. Jesus declared in the temple that the Spirit of the Lord was upon Him, and He was the Anointed One who is the fulfillment of the prophecy. His life, crucifixion, resurrection and ascension fulfilled the prophecy (Luke 4:18).

Jesus sent His disciples out to preach the kingdom of heaven is at hand, and to demonstrate His authority by healing the sick, cleansing the lepers, raising the dead, and delivering people from demonic oppression and spiritual bondage. They had experienced the superior reality of the kingdom of heaven in their own lives; therefore, they were qualified and deployed as Christ's followers to lead others into freedom and their true God-given identities (Matthew 10:7-8).

In the Great Commission, Jesus implored His followers to make disciples of all nations, baptizing them in the name of the Father, Son, and Holy Spirit. He charged the disciples to teach converts to follow all that He had commanded them, and to never forget He was with them always (Matthew 28:18-20).

In John 21, the resurrected Jesus is eating breakfast with the disciples. He turns to Peter, and asks, "Do you love me?" three times. To which Peter replies "yes" each time. Jesus tells Peter that if he loves Him, he will "feed My lambs", "tend My sheep", and "feed My sheep." Jesus is saying to Peter, if you love me, you will treasure what I treasure - all of humankind, who the Father made in His image.

Jesus restored creation's entanglement relationship with its Creator. As new creations in Christ, we are His ambassadors who represent Him wherever we go. We know Him by the spirit instead of the flesh. The old covenant gave way to the new. Jesus's death on the Cross and resurrection from the grave provides grace for salvation and empowers us to live according to our identities as sons and daughters of a loving Father.

As His ambassadors, it is our privilege and responsibility to feed His lambs and tend His sheep. Just as Jesus did not come to be served, but to serve others, we get to do the same. Being the hands and feet of Jesus compels those whom we serve to receive God's love.

One experience with God's love has the power to magnify the sound of Jesus knocking at the door of a person's heart, who would have otherwise not heard Him. If that person will answer the door and let Him in, He will dine with them for eternity (Revelation 3:20). This is how the kingdom of heaven expands throughout the earth; it expands through the hearts of humanity.

Maxwell stated that "every atom of creation is unfathomable in its perfection." Perhaps there comes a point where we explore creation so deeply that the irrefutable truth is revealed that there is a God, and He is our Creator. Perhaps science is actually unveiling the mysteries of heaven on earth, and Christ with us, even at the hands of individuals who have yet to see themselves as children of God, but are unknowingly building upon Maxwell's Holy Spirit-led foundation.

Why do I share all of this with you? Because it's important to recognize that our modern tech space was founded on the principle of partnering with the Holy Spirit to pull ideas from the hidden realm to the natural world. And yet, the church isn't typically associated with this type of innovation, even though we have the mind of Christ and are called to be His manifold wisdom.

What if the unlocking of the next epoch in tech innovation is accelerated by the next generation of Maxwells, who partner with God to pull innovations from the invisible heavenly realm into our physical world? What if these innovations are fully actualized by using them how God designed them, to help people and lead them to an encounter with Christ? I propose that we would see a revival to and through the tech space in which all would encounter the goodness of God and know Him as Lord. The key to all of it is desiring what Jesus desires, and partnering with Him to bring heaven on earth.

My hope is that the next generation of Spirit-led Maxwells will rise up and reveal that science is a gift from God that reveals His plan for Creation through new discoveries and innovation such as quantum computing. But you don't have to be adept in quantum computing to usher in the next epoch. You just have to listen to God's voice, trust what He is asking you to do with Him, and do what He's saying to pull solutions from the invisible realm into the natural world. Technology will be a tool you can use to make it happen, whether it already exists or God is calling you to create it with Him.

7

A MOONSHOT FACTORY

"Jesus looked at them and said, 'With man this is impossible, but with God all things are possible.'" Matthew 19:26 NIV

Not far from the sprawling Google headquarters in Mountain View, CA, in what was once an old cavernous shopping mall, now sits a moonshot factory. This is what Google calls its innovation lab (Google X) because of its mission to achieve the impossible for the good of humanity. The name was inspired by President John F. Kennedy's speech in 1962. In it he told the world we will put a man on the moon by the end of the decade, "not because it is easy, but because it is hard."[92]

It is this factory that birthed the ideas for self-driving cars (Waymo) and delivery service drones (Wing). The premise behind Google's moonshot factory is to create radical technologies that solve the world's hardest problems through moonshot ideas. For X, anyone can take a moonshot, regardless of their background or education. The only requirement is a commitment to wildly pursue the impossible to solve a problem that impacts the world for good.

Moonshot thinking is about going after the things that sound unattainable, but if done, propel humanity forward. Or, according to X, a moonshot has the potential to even redefine humanity.

The greatest innovators function in the realm of the impossible. Maxwell, Faraday, Thomson, and Babbage understood this and formed a Holy Spirit-led moonshot season that serves as the foundation for technological innovation to this day.

Sadly, the Body of Christ didn't keep the momentum going, but there is no reason the Church can't reignite the Holy Spirit-led innovation that marked their lives and discoveries 150 years ago. The Church is designed to be a moonshot factory, appropriating Jesus's "why" wherever we go and pulling heavenly solutions into the physical world.

In Ephesians 3:10, Paul calls on the Church to put on full display the manifold wisdom of God, which was made available to us through Jesus, in whom all things were created. This superior wisdom is not only for the physical world, but is also to be unveiled by the Church to the principalities and powers in the heavenly places.

We are containers of heaven everywhere we go. Let that sink in because that understanding is not Christianese thrown around flippantly to elicit "Praise the Lords" and "Hallelujahs" in a Sunday morning church service. This is our very identity: heirs of God, co-heirs with Christ, and re-presenters of His authority. The Holy Spirit within us bears witness to this truth (Romans 8:16).

God embedded a moonshot mentality in all of humankind because He made us in His image. And He is the brilliant Creator of the universe. There is a desire in every person's heart to look at the physical world and search for the invisible attributes of creation that will move humanity closer to its Creator (Romans 1:20).

On its website, Google X outlines tips to develop a moonshot mindset. Most of them are Kingdom values, without being identified as such. In the same way there is correlation between Bethel Tech's high-character Kingdom values and the soft-skills companies are investing millions of dollars to improve workplace culture, there are incredible parallels between the mindset X has outlined to achieve the impossible and God's invitation for His children to innovate with the Holy Spirit.

Inspired by Google X, I've built a list of core values for a Holy Spirit-led innovator. The Body of Christ is designed to be a moonshot factory that actualizes Divine solutions from the invisible realm to solve every earthly problem that is in violation with the superior reality of the kingdom of heaven. I encourage you to use this list as a guidepost to innovate with God, achieve the impossible, and move humanity heavenward.

1. Fall in love with the problem and the people it's affecting

This is an iteration of Google X's moonshot tip: Fall in love with the problem. And, it goes back to my question, "why do you even want to teleport?" If the answer doesn't move humanity heavenward, the pursuit will always end up less than its God-intended purpose.

One of my favorite phrases in the Bible is, "Then, Jesus was moved with compassion." Immediately following this phrase, we see Jesus heal the sick, cast out demons, raise the dead, and share the good news to the brokenhearted and set them free. (Matthew 14:13-14; Matthew 20:30-34; Luke 7:12-15; Mark 6:34; Mark 1:41; Matthew 8:16)

As Christ's ambassadors, this should be our core value as well. Technology is a tool, not the solution. Jesus is the solution that is magnified through the use of technology.

The moment we spend more time focusing on how great the tool is, we shift our focus from "heaven to earth" to "earth to heaven." Brick by brick, that perspective becomes a vain attempt to build a new tower of Babel to replace the kingdom of heaven. What a sad realization to stand before the throne of God one day, having spent a lifetime, trying to build a stairway to heaven, only to find out the address was within a whisper's distance, placed inside the heart of all humans. The path is as easy as opening the door and letting Jesus, the Kingdom of Heaven, inside.

Scott Harrison is the founder of Charity: water, and his story is incredible. You can read the full story in his book *Thirst*, but the short of it is Scott was a former nightclub promoter in New York City, indulging in the dark vices of the NYC club scene. He got in some trouble with the wrong person, who showed up at his apartment with a gun, and he had to flee New York City for his life.

As an escape, and wanting to help people in need, Scott volunteered as a photographer with Mercy Ships, a Christian non-profit organization that travels around the world and provides life-saving surgeries to people in developing countries. Seeing first-hand the rampant malnutrition and lack of resources in the communities Mercy Ships helped, he discovered that water-related diseases are responsible for 80 percent of all illnesses and deaths in developing countries. Furthermore, there were over a billion people in these countries who did not have access to clean drinking water.

Scott gave his life to Christ, and set out on a moonshot journey to make sure everyone across the globe had access to clean water. In 15 years since its launch, Charity: water has funded over 91 thousand water projects, drilling fresh water wells in developing countries and serving nearly 15 million people in over 29 countries. They place IoT (Internet of Things) sensors on their water pipes that can monitor whether or not fresh, clean water is appropriately flowing through the wells. If the data from the sensors reveals a lack of water flow, Charity: water has local boots on the ground to correct the problem.

In his book, Scott shares a story of a woman who would wake up at dawn every day, walk a mile and a half with a jug on her head to the nearest water point, and wait in line for hours with other women to collect water. Charity: water drilled a fresh-water well in her community, allowing her and her family access to clean water. "Now I have time to eat, and my children can go to school," she shared with Scott's team.

When we provide a tangible source of hope, hope actually starts to take shape, and a healthy community begins to materialize. For the woman in the story and her family, removing the opportunity cost of spending all day retrieving water meant her children could go to school, and she had time to eat. Their old ceiling in life became a new floor upon which they could learn, grow, thrive and create legacy.

Scott had compassion on the people he saw being devastated by unclean water, and he was compelled to do something about it. For Scott, the statistics were sobering.

But to see a young child on the verge of death because of a lack of clean water, as Scott would often witness on the Mercy Ship, was heart-breaking, and it compelled him to take action. Falling in love with the people who are being affected by a problem creates the highest sense of ownership to find an ultimate solution.

In his book, *Built to Last: Successful Habits of Visionary Companies*, Jim Collins calls this "the big hairy audacious goal" (BHAG). A BHAG inspires others to pursue the impossible, turning a moonshot into reality because it goes beyond pro formas and balance sheets. The idea itself energizes and raises the standard of what a person and group of people believe is possible.

A Kingdom-minded BHAG, like Charity: water's moonshot, is the catalytic motion of bringing heaven to earth. Jesus said, "If you abide in Me, and My words abide in you, you will ask what you desire and it shall be done for you. By this My Father is glorified, that you bear much fruit; so you will be My disciples." (John 15:7-8 NKJV)

Being a disciple of God is evident in the heavenly fruit we bear on earth. Every good and perfect gift comes from our loving Father (James 1:17). As bearers of His good and perfect fruit, our minimum expectation as the Body of Christ is to give a fish to those in need, so to speak. But our ideal expectation is to set them up to learn how to fish so they can create a legacy within their families for generations to come.

This is the path Charity: water creates by providing access to clean drinking water. Scott and his team are bringing freedom to the broken-hearted, setting the captives free, providing hope and good news to the poor, healing the sick and delivering entire communities from the devil's stronghold of death and destruction. And they are using technological innovation to make it happen.

2. Go and be light

We are called to shine the light of Jesus before others, so that they may see our good works and glorify our Father in heaven (Matthew 5:16). The manifestation of God's goodness in our lives draws others into an encounter with Him.

Jesus said greater works than you've seen me do, you will do because I ascend to my Father in heaven (John 14:12). Might I remind you, Jesus healed the sick, raised the dead, cast out demons, turned water into wine, multiplied five loaves and two fish to feed five thousand (and then again with four thousand), walked through walls, walked on water, and instantly transported from a boat to the other side of a lake. These were all the manifestations of His moonshot to rescue humanity from the fate of sin and restore our right-standing relationship with our loving Father for eternity.

The Body of Christ was not intended to isolate itself within the confines of a building or hide its light under a basket, as the first part of Matthew 5:16 states. We are called to go and be the light to everyone, everywhere, including the tech space. Darkness must give way to light wherever light is present.

In Matthew 10, Jesus gathered His 12 disciples and gave them power over unclean spirits and to heal the sick. Then He sent them out, imploring them to *go* and preach that the kingdom of heaven is at hand. He instructed them to heal the sick, cleanse the lepers, raise the dead and cast out demons. Freely He gave them the power of the Kingdom so they could freely release it to others (Matthew 10:7-8).

A few years ago, I began traveling a lot for work. I started taking Uber trips on a regular basis, and the Lord told me I was going to be a light in the darkness for my Uber drivers. The very first trip I took, the driver recommitted her life to the Lord!

To be candid, I'm not one who loves getting into vulnerable conversations with strangers. I also feel incredibly uncomfortable with the very setting of an Uber trip. I'm basically putting a high level of trust in a stranger to safely drive me to my destination. The last thing I want to do is push them into a state of anxiety or emotional distress with a heavy conversation around the struggles in their lives.

But leading them to an encounter with Jesus is worth the risk. To ease into the conversation, I'll usually start by asking who they voted for in the last presidential election.

The driver who recommitted her life to the Lord had experienced a horrible divorce in which her husband, who was a pastor, had an affair with another woman and ran off with her. The driver was left to raise two young boys on her own.

The church came to the aid of her husband to restore him, but she felt like they treated her like an outcast. She hadn't been back to church since.

I told her God loves her and sees her, and that His heart broke when she was treated unfairly by her husband. I told her I was so sorry that was how she experienced the church, but that was not God. I prayed for her to experience the embrace of God's love, and she did right in the car! With tears in her eyes, she told God she was tired of running from Him, and she committed to running to Him every day of her life. I recommended a couple of great churches in the area that I knew would embrace her as a child of God.

Then I prayed Jeremiah 29:11 over her sons. I declared God's plans and promises to give them a hope and future would be so evident in their lives, they would be overwhelmed with the goodness of God, and give their lives to Him as well.

As we approached my destination, the driver told me she had been feeling extra low that day, and almost rejected my Uber request on the app. But something inside of her told her she needed to accept it. Right after I got out of the car, she thanked me and said her life was forever changed because of our conversation.

Since then, I've had incredible conversations with Uber drivers, in which they've given their lives to God, received confirmation or clarity on direction for their future, and broken free from guilt and shame. God often will give me a specific verse for them to lean on and, on many occasions, they've echoed what my first Uber driver said: "I was in a very low place today, and was going to reject your Uber request. But something inside me told me I needed to accept it."

A couple of months ago, I had an Uber driver say that same thing to me. And, man, was he ever in a low place. He was in such a bad emotional state, I was legitimately concerned for my safety. It's possible he was driving under the influence of a chemical substance, but I'm certain he was driving under the influence of a demonic spirit of depression.

When I got into the car, he asked me how I was doing, but I could tell he really wanted me to ask how he was doing. So, I did.

Then, he proceeded to tell me he had recently lost his job, and he caught his girlfriend cheating on him... in the act. He left nothing to the imagination in his description, and went on a tirade about how much he hated her and her teenage son. Then he told me he had just gotten out of jail, and it was at that time I couldn't help but remember the circular saw in the trunk of his car when I loaded up my suitcase. I was 10 minutes into a 30-minute trip, but it felt like a hellish eternity.

Meanwhile, the driver kept missing turns and going in the opposite direction of my destination. He had Uber maps guiding him, but he paid no attention to it. I had to direct him with every turn, and it was like he wasn't even there. I was about to ask him to pull over, so I could get out, but the Lord reminded me that I carry His presence and superior reality in the situation.

So, I started praying under my breath, and then I asked the driver if I could pray for him. He said yes, and by the end of the prayer, his entire countenance changed. It was like he was a different person. I felt the Lord tell me to pray over his ex-girlfriend, the one who cheated on him, and I called her a daughter of God, whom God loved deeply. That's when I saw a drastic improvement in his demeanor.

By then we had arrived at my destination, but God wasn't done. I continued to speak life and truth over the driver, and then I heard the Lord say to pray for the driver's estranged children from a previous relationship. That's when he started to cry.

He asked me how I knew he had children. I told him God had told me, and then the driver told me he had children whom he hadn't spoken to in years. I told him God was going to bring restoration to his relationship with his children, and that today was the beginning of significant change in his life. I asked him if he had received Jesus as his Lord and Savior, and he said he had years ago. He let out a light chuckle and told me he had met his ex-girlfriend while he was volunteering for his church.

I encouraged him to spend time with God when I got out of the car and have a deep, unfiltered conversation with Him. I gave him a verse and told him the next five minutes will shape the rest of His life, because God was going to provide him a path that will lead him out of despair into a hope-filled future.

I've found that, when I step out in bold faith to pray for someone on the spot, something shifts in the atmosphere. Someone who is seemingly unreceptive to God or listening to His voice will open up in vulnerability and receive prayer.

Before Uber, I rarely used taxi services. It felt like too much work and money to reserve one, unless I was downtown in a large city, like New York or Chicago. But the ease of use through Uber's ride share app on my smart phone, near-immediate access to an available driver, and low-cost fares shifted my perspective. Uber served as a disruptive technology that God used to create a unique mission field for me to share the gospel of Jesus.

As God's heirs and co-heirs with Christ, we are containers of the kingdom of heaven, who enact His superior reality wherever we go. Any inferior reality has to obey the superior reality of Jesus. When we do this, we prepare the atmosphere for people to encounter the goodness of God, which is the catalyst to repentance. Again, not out of compliance, but out of the peace and joy that passes all understanding when people get a glimpse into how much God loves and cares about them as His children. This is true in every situation, setting, and sphere – including the tech space.

My friend Sue Warnke exemplifies what it looks like to be the light of Jesus in the tech space better than anyone I've ever seen. Sue is a senior director at Salesforce, one of the leading tech companies in the world, and she has an incredible testimony of salvation, which you can read in detail on her website: Leanership.org.[93]

On the surface, Sue had it all—an incredible family and an amazing job at one of the most influential tech companies in Silicon Valley. Yet, she knew something in her life was missing.

On a business trip, the sense of void bubbled over for Sue. Alone in her hotel room, she said to herself, "I give up." She didn't realize it at the time, but the Lord's strength is made perfect in our weakness (2 Corinthians 12:9), and her words were actually a powerful act of surrender that unlocked her ability to hear Jesus knocking on her heart's door. Through a series of Divine experiences over the next few weeks she gave her life to Jesus.

First, her son's doctor gave her a medical article that talked about the healing power of God. Then, an image of her kids' old karate teacher popped into her head. She recalled how good he was with his students, and she remembered he had invited her to church one time six years ago.

She called him, and asked if the offer still stood. The next Sunday she went to church with him, and let people pray for her. A day later, she traveled to Austin, TX for a business trip, and when she got to her hotel room, she received a text from the karate teacher that said, "Without you totally understanding what I mean, I pray that the 'Holy Spirit'

(God) reveals to you what He revealed to me almost 30 years ago."[94]

Moments after she read the text, Sue's aunt called her and shared the good news of Jesus with her. Sue listened to her aunt, believed and received the gift of Salvation.

Sue received Jesus, and couldn't help but be the light to everyone around her. With a few other believers, she founded Faithforce, the first faith-based Employee Resource Group (ERG) at Salesforce, as well as Christians@Salesforce.

I've had the opportunity to visit Sue at work a couple of times, and it's common for people to stop her in the lobby or in the elevator and thank her for sharing Jesus with them. I remember a security guard thanking her for setting up an Easter Service at Salesforce, and how it changed his life. Sue hosted a church service at the HQ of a Tech giant in Silicon Valley!

With over a thousand members, Faithforce is one of the fastest growing ERGs at Salesforce, and CEO Marc Benioff even shared about Sue and Faithforce in his book, *Trailblazer*.

Sue speaks at conferences in Silicon Valley and across the country, sharing her testimony and providing practical ways believers can create faith groups like Faithforce at their companies. She reminds me so much of the Apostle Paul, who upon his conversion on the road to Damascus wasted no time sharing his Jesus testimony with the world and leading people to an encounter with the love of Christ.

As Christ-followers, we have full confidence knowing that Jesus is the way, truth and life. He is not broken, and does not need to be improved. We can boldly proclaim the truth of Jesus in our words and actions, re-presenting Love Personified to everyone, everywhere. Knowing who Truth is, we should be looking for every opportunity to enact His power and authority wherever we go. Just like Sue does.

When we keep ourselves locked in our lab (church building), we limit our ability to co-labor with God to expand His church beyond an inclusive subculture. Meanwhile, the multitudes are crying out for help, needing the very Jesus we keep to ourselves within our church walls.

Please hear me: it is so important to find a great church home. There's something special about being together as a community of believers connecting with each other and worshiping Jesus together. I encourage you to find a life-giving church, rooted in the Word of God and focused on representing the love of Christ.

Because Sue Warnke was the light of Jesus wherever she went, she didn't just expand the walls of the church; she knocked the walls down and brought the church to a space that isn't supposed to be receptive to Jesus. The moonshot emanating from Sue's good works is that all would experience the glorious love of our heavenly Father, and the church would cover the globe in every sphere of society.

In Jesus's parable of the talents, He compares the kingdom of heaven to a man traveling to a far country, who assigned His financial management to His servants (Matthew 25:14-30). To one He gave five talents; to another He gave two talents; and to the third servant He gave one. He gave to each according to his ability.

The servant with five talents *immediately* went out and doubled His investment. The one with two talents *immediately* did the same. But the servant with one talent dug a hole in the ground and hid the Master's money.

When the Master returned, He took inventory of how His

servants stewarded his accounts. To the first two servants who immediately invested and doubled the money, the Master responded, "Well done, good and faithful servant; you have been faithful over a few things, I will make you ruler over many things." (Matthew 25: 21, 23 NKJV)

But, to the servant who hid the money and didn't invest, the Master responded, "You wicked and lazy servant, you knew that I reap where I have not sown, and gather where I have not scattered seed." (Matthew 25:26 NKJV) The Master then took the one talent from the unfaithful servant and disbursed it to the servant who doubled the five.

God's Word and promises will not return void. I want to pose a sobering question to the Body of Christ: What if the Big "C" church is not using all of its resources to steward its talents, and in some ways is like the servant who hid the investment in a hole in the ground?

As Christ's ambassadors, we are called fishers of men. But what if there are multiple ways to fish? For some it's a pole. For others it's a net.

What I'm getting at is: technology is another way to fish. By not engaging the tech space, the Church has relinquished its authority in the most influential sphere of society. Meanwhile, the tech space is ripe with moonshot thinkers who have built companies that have changed the world. In fact, 7 of the top 8 most valuable companies in the world are tech companies, many of which have a massive impact on people's daily lives:[95]

Apple (#1)
Microsoft (#2)
Alphabet/Google (#3)

Amazon (#5)
Tesla (#6)
Meta/Facebook (#7)
NVIDIA (#8)

It is easy to see the leaders of these companies operating in their God-given gifts and talents, even if they don't realize the source of their giftings. Remember, every person was created by God on purpose and for a purpose with specific abilities that reveal His creativity and goodness.

It is a travesty when a person never receives his or her identity as son or daughter of God. The gifts and talents evident in their lives are never fully actualized if they are not used in partnership with God to bring humanity heavenward.

However, it's also a travesty when believers sell themselves and God short by not operating as Holy Spirit-led moonshot-takers who reveal the goodness of God from glory to glory through mind-blowing Divine solutions. It is imperative that the Body of Christ answer the call to bring the kingdom of heaven to the world instead of waiting for the world to come to our idea labs.

3. Win together. Lose alone.

Humanity is woven together through relationships and diversity of voices. We are a beautiful mosaic that unveils a breathtaking picture of Jesus when we are fully present and connected. To exclude a voice is to deprive humanity of the full breadth of the beauty of Creation. God imagined humankind, and made us in His image. We, collectively, are the full Body of Christ and represent His manifold wisdom on earth as it is in heaven.

The Apostle Paul wrote to the Church of Ephesus that his passion was to enlighten every person to the divine mystery of the incomprehensible riches of Christ for the purpose of unveiling God's manifold (full and diverse) wisdom through the church. The word manifold in Ephesians 3:10 is the same word used to describe Joseph's coat of manifold (or diverse) colors in Genesis 37:3.

Imagine having the power to fully actualize the full wisdom of the Creator of the universe. Does that seem too hard to imagine? Good, you are not meant to carry that responsibility alone. But, it can and will be achieved in partnership with the Holy Spirit and with your brothers and sisters in Christ.

I tell our Bethel Tech team that it's easy to lose when you try to do things on your own, but no one ever wins alone. Success is a result of collaboration, teamwork, and diversity of thought which should be highlighted and celebrated in all we do.

One of the most important things the Lord did for me in starting Bethel Tech was bring the right people to help build the foundation of our school. Johanna Wilson is a great example.

Two months into building the framework of our school, largely on my own, I desperately needed a high-capacity operations person (OPS) to run with. Not just a high-capacity OPS person, but a high-capacity OPS person in the area of online higher education.

I interviewed a number of people, but none of them were experienced in the nuances that come with higher education programs. To boot, my funnel was small because the person had to live in Redding, a small city in Northern California, not known as a large higher education market.

In a leadership meeting at Bethel one morning, I asked if anyone knew of someone who had a lot of experience in higher education operations. Our pastor-on-call leader came up to me after the meeting, and said he had someone who was volunteering for his department.

He sent me Johanna's resume, and her experience and qualifications seemed too good to be true. I purposely wrote the job description to scare away the faint of heart because I knew I needed someone to run with, not someone I had to micromanage. I needed someone who was well-versed in the things I wasn't, specifically related to higher education regulations and compliance.

When I interviewed her, Johanna could verify all her experience and her skills. I hired her on the spot.

The beauty of Johanna's story is that she had over 15 years of online higher education operations experience, but was currently working as a director of a lake resort near Redding. Because of an unfortunate situation with her last education employer, in which the CEO was secretly making unethical business decisions behind her back, the company folded and she lost what she thought was her dream job in education.

Johanna is more passionate about higher education and more committed to running operations as a way to represent Jesus than anyone I've ever met. While I was praying for God to bring someone to help me build Bethel Tech, Johanna was praying for God to bring her back into a higher education role that also allowed her to stay in Redding.

The Bible says one can chase a thousand and two can put ten thousand to flight (Deuteronomy 32:30). I can't think of a

more appropriate verse to describe the Lord bringing
Johanna to Bethel Tech.

When we step out in faith and pioneer with God, He is
faithful to bring people together who are aligned in mission
and vision to manifest His will on earth as it is in heaven.
God met an individual need for me and an individual need
for Johanna as part of His masterplan to transform thousands
of people's lives through Bethel Tech.

God takes His faithfulness to the one son or daughter and
combines them together to reveal His moonshot that none
should perish, but receive the gift of salvation through Jesus.
From this grace of salvation, we enter into an ongoing
eternal, personal relationship with Him, which empowers us
to actualize our God-given callings.

We can no longer try to bring heaven to earth alone,
fragmented and fractured by denominational, economical,
geographical, and ethnic divides. Technology and modern
communication networks, like the internet and social media,
should, in theory, bring everyone closer together.
Unfortunately, that hasn't been the case. The devil has
perverted it and turned it into a pretty little hate machine,
creating echo chambers to create further division within
humanity.

Again, technology is a tool that takes on the function of its
user. If I gave you a hammer, you could build a house, but
you could also use it as a weapon to crack someone over the
head.

In 2016, Microsoft launched a Twitter account that was
completely run by an AI bot called "Tay". The bot would
take on a personality and post tweets based on its
engagement with other human-run accounts and data

collection from their tweets on the social media platform. Within 24 hours Tay turned into a hate machine, spewing out vile diatribes, and Microsoft had to shut it down.

Left to our own devices, technology and the ability to communicate a message globally and instantly with a push of a button can be a scary thing. The lack of accountability has created a pretend reality in which people operate from a false sense of identity, creating a virtual version of themselves. In the virtual dream, individuals can say and do whatever they want behind the protective barrier of their device screens, with little to no accountability for how their actions affect others. The time has come for the full Body of Christ to flip the script and move together in unity, making "every effort to keep the unity of the Spirit through the bond of peace." (Ephesians 4:3-6 NIV)

4. Embrace ~~failure~~ learning

This one is straight from Google X:

> "Fail fast" has become a Silicon Valley cliché. But let's admit it: people hate failing. Society has conditioned us to see failure as something shameful and best to be avoided at all costs. The thing is, though, taking moonshots isn't possible without failing a few times along the way. The trick is to create a culture that makes it psychologically safe for people to fail, and reframes each failure as an opportunity to learn. Once you start celebrating your team's failures as much as its successes, valuing each mistake for its lessons, you'll be surprised to see how quickly audacity can become the path of least resistance.[96]

Our failures don't define us, unless we let them keep us down or cause us to quit what God has called us to do. God's grace is sufficient for us in all things (2 Corinthians 12:9), and it empowers us to live out the purpose God placed on our lives.

When we step out into new territory we may not always get everything right the first time. But motive matters. If we don't give up, we will see the fruit (Galatians 6:9). God's not looking for perfection. He's looking for a willing, surrendered and obedient heart.

I often wonder if God looks at some of the paths we forge in technology, and thinks to Himself, "Interesting they decided to go that direction." I touched on the differences between classical computing and quantum computing earlier in the book. We know that quantum computing represents a far superior computing process than classical, and we've had the foundation of quantum computing (with quantum mechanics) for over a century. When we finally fully actualize its potential, and it points to God as Creator, I wonder if God will be like "What took you so long?"

Bill Johnson often shares the following example of the disciples turning a failure into an opportunity to explore and understand the kingdom of heaven at a deeper level. In Matthew 17, we find a man asking Jesus to heal his demon-possessed son. The man first brought his son to Jesus's disciples, but they were unable to heal him. Jesus cast out the demon, and the boy was immediately cured.

This happened *after* Jesus commissioned His disciples to cast out demons and heal the sick, which they did and reported all the miracles they had seen in the places they went. Instead of sulking in their failure and disqualifying themselves from their calling, the disciples leaned into learning from Jesus. They came to Jesus privately and asked why they could not cast out the demon.

In that moment, they learned the power of faith and the consequence of unbelief. Jesus told them if they had unrelenting faith as tiny as a mustard seed, they could move mountains, and nothing would be impossible for them. One iota of faith in the kingdom of heaven is more powerful than all of the strength and brainpower of humanity combined.

On paper, the disciples didn't appear qualified to be in Jesus's inner circle. Just looking at them, they didn't seem to be the ones who would start His church and make disciples of all nations.

The disciples were a rag-tag group from the lower working class, including fishermen and a tax collector. Their disciple resumes wouldn't have made it through the first qualification algorithm on Indeed.com.

But God has a habit of using the "unqualified," so long as their desires mirror His desires, and they are profoundly aware that they cannot accomplish the calling apart from Him. We see it throughout the Bible. Moses had an almost paralyzing fear of public speaking. Yet, God chose him to stand up to Pharaoh, ruler of the most powerful empire in the world at the time, and deliver the Israelites from Egyptian captivity.

Rahab was a prostitute, who God used to hide the spies in Jericho so the Israelites could take the Promised Land. The Israelites spared her when they destroyed Jericho, and they took her in as one of their own. She ended up being the great grandmother to King David and part of Jesus's genealogy.

David too appeared unqualified on paper. He was a little shepherd boy and the youngest of his brothers. When the

Prophet Samuel came to his house to anoint the next king of Israel, David's father, Jesse, didn't even consider offering him as a candidate.

Samuel needed a little Divine correction in the process. When the prophet saw Jesse's son, Eliab, he said, "Surely the Lord's anointed is before Him!" But the Lord said to Samuel, "Do not look at his appearance or at his physical stature, because I have refused him. For the Lord does not see as man sees; for man looks at the outward appearance, but the Lord looks at the heart." (I Samuel 16:6-7 NKJV)

Jesse brought in David last, only after Samuel asked if there were any more sons other than the first seven. When David entered the house, the Lord said, "This is the one!" David went on to become the greatest king Israel had ever seen.

And there was Paul, who before his conversion on the road to Damascus, imprisoned and condemned Christians to death for following Jesus. After his conversion, Paul became the great apostle, writing two-thirds of the New Testament.

The disciples were trailblazers taking new territory for the kingdom of heaven. They had no blueprint, other than to trust in Jesus, which in reality is the only blueprint needed to manifest heaven on earth.

I love how C.S. Lewis said it in *Mere Christianity*: "Look for Christ, and you will find Him. And with Him, everything else." From the perspective of utter dependence on God, being unqualified is a valuable asset. All moonshot-takers are unqualified at some point because they are attempting to do something that has never been done before.

The disciples' failure in the situation with the demon-possessed boy opened a door for them to go deeper in their dependency to God. And it was this learning opportunity that prepared them to build the early Church.

With Bethel Tech, we did a lot of things well from the start. I attribute this to the Lord directing our path and bringing the right people together, who listen and obey what the Lord is saying. The members of our team are not just hearers of the Word, they go and do what He is telling them to do.

Having said that, there were areas where we thought we would succeed, but didn't. So, we pivoted. These situations were not failures, or even problems. Rather, they were learning opportunities for us to grow.

The best piece of advice my mentor and Bethel Tech co-founder, Kris Vallotton, ever gave me had to do with what I perceived as a massive failure at the time. We were about a year into our school, and had a partner that was responsible for paying us a large portion of our tuition revenue. Because of some extenuating circumstances and improper execution of the partner agreement, the partner was not paying us tuition. That caused us to not be able to pay our systems and platform-provider on time. We were at risk of our students getting locked out of their courses.

I walked into our board meeting, having just received a final notice from our systems vendor that they were going to shut our service down the following week if we didn't square up our bill. This is in no way to disparage our vendor. They are a business that operates by getting paid on time for the services they deliver. As do we.

Nevertheless, I was shaken and visibly upset, trying to hold it together to run the meeting. Kris turned to me and said, "See me in my office after this meeting."

I was sure I was about to get my butt handed to me, and I knew I deserved it. But Kris sat me down, and asked what was wrong. I unloaded in full detail the mess we were in, and how I felt like such a failure.

"This isn't a problem," he responded. And there was a supernatural confidence to his words and demeanor that brought me peace and security. Kris has been through the fire countless times in his life, and he has come out better and wiser on the other side because of his utter dependence on God. When you are a Holy Spirit-led pioneer like Kris, you're bound to be forged in the fire often. I knew if he said it wasn't a problem, it wasn't a problem. And you know what? It wasn't.

We got through the issue and strengthened our relationship with our system provider at the time. We lost money from the partner who owed us tuition money, but we learned how to better execute a Service Level Agreement (SLA) with future partners and what to look for in a healthy business partner. And our school continued to grow!

We've since had other difficult situations, as all startups and established organizations do, but I have committed to adopting Kris's perspective that these aren't problems. They are opportunities to partner with God to materialize Divine solutions from heaven to earth, and there is beauty in learning from situations where we don't hit our target. It's only a failure if we don't learn from it and course-correct to the right path.

5. Become a chaos pilot

This one is also straight from Google X, and I absolutely love it!

> Taking moonshots is no smooth sailing. It's an inherently
> unpredictable and bumpy ride. Rather than shy away from
> the uncertainty, it's best to just embrace it. That means
> challenging yourself to stare into the unknown and instead
> of being paralyzed by it, seeing it as a source of creative
> energy and momentum. The sooner you decide to surf the
> chaos, the easier the chaos gets — and could even be used
> to your advantage.[97]

I believe the Church is not averse to hard work. Where I see
the Church get squeamish is in the land of the unfamiliar. The
chaos of the unknown is often enough for the Church not to
engage all spheres of influence, including the tech space.

Jesus warned us that in this world there will be trials and
tribulations, challenges and inevitable chaos that will seek to
steal our peace and replace it with fear. But He said, be of
good cheer, for I have overcome the world (John 16:33). Our
peace comes from His Spirit inside our hearts, and not from
circumstances around us, because greater is He who is in us
than he who is in this world (1 John 4:4).

When we set out to do something that's never been done,
there is bound to be resistance. The truth is most people
would rather fall in line than create the line for others to
follow.

Gary Starkweather was a junior engineer at the Xerox
Corporation in the 1960s when he started working on a
photocopier that could transmit information between copiers
in different locations. He realized the best way to do this was
through laser beams that produced precise images, which he

believed would be exponentially higher in quality than the images currently produced by Xerox photocopiers. In 1971, Starkweather invented the laser printer, allowing the transfer and print of high-quality images from printer to printer and computer to printer.[98] Today, you can find his invention in homes and offices across the world.

"What you have to do is not just look at the marble," he shared in a presentation to a class at the University of South Florida in 2017. "You have to see the angel in the marble."[99] The statement no doubt was an homage to the greatest and most innovative sculptor of the Italian Renaissance, Michelangelo, who said, "I saw the angel in the marble and carved until I set him free."

This is what innovators do. They use their imagination to see what others don't, and make the impossible a reality.

Starkweather, who passed away in December 2019, was greatly inspired by Faraday and Maxwell. And like both of them, he believed the more time we spent with God and explored His creation, the more He would reveal His creativity to and through us. The "discoverability of our world," as Starkweather put it, and the exercise of creating with God is an act of worship that uncovers the great depths of God's love for humanity.[100]

Given that Starkweather worked for Xerox, one of the most creative and technologically advanced companies of that time, you'd think his innovation would have been welcomed with open arms. But that wasn't the case.

His boss hated the idea. He saw "lasers" as a sci-fi fantasy with no practical use, and he told Starkweather he would be fired if he didn't stop working on the project.

So, Starkweather moved from Rochester, New York to

Palo Alto, CA (Silicon Valley), and secretly worked on the project at Xerox's Palo Alto Research Center (PARC) with a design team who also created the Alto computer that was compatible to send images to Starkweather's machine for print.

"One of the goals of the Alto was to build a computer that could work with images that were as flexible as those made with all the tools of graphics arts that had been developed over the previous 500 years," Butler Lampson, founder of the Alto project, recalled. "We made it possible to do that on the screen. And Gary made it possible to take the information on the screen and put it onto paper."[101]

Later, Steve Jobs, founder of Apple, would visit Xerox, and use the Alto as inspiration to build the Apple Macintosh computer. Xerox could have dominated the computer market by leaning into its computing innovation with the Alto, but instead it chose to stick with its tried and true core business - the photocopier. Jobs picked up where Xerox left off, and Apple became a worldwide leader in computing technology and consumer electronics. Xerox could have been Apple, but fell trap to the comfort and familiarity of the status quo.

All innovation requires chaos. For Bethel Tech, we cast a vision of equipping Kingdom-minded believers with in-demand tech skills to enter the marketplace. When we started classes, we had to deliver what we said we would. In some ways it felt like jumping off a tall building with a hang glider and putting it together in mid-air. Innovating or starting something that's never been done before will always feel this way, no matter how well you prepare.

There is certain insight that can only come from putting yourself out there for the world to experience, and then gleaning insight from their experience of your product. It can be exciting, but also exhausting to live in that state of unfamiliarity.

In theory, we'd all love to learn everything we need to know first, and then go do the new thing flawlessly. But the reality is that you learn, then do, then learn from doing and iterate, and do some more.

And on and on this cycle goes. The best learning is on-the-job, thrown-into-the arena, drinking-from-a firehose, real-life experience.

Innovative founders often thrive in chaos because they are dreamers who see the angel in the marble where others just see a huge rock. But the peril of success is that it can lead people and companies to rest on their laurels.

Oftentimes, it's the day-to-day management of operating a core part of a business driven by balance sheets and P&L statements that takes up all of an organization's focus. I can attest to this with Bethel Tech. When you have a vision for something, it's an incredible feeling to see that vision turn into a reality. But once you take your product or service to market, a whole litany of new responsibilities take shape.

Before long, if you're not careful, creative dreaming sessions take a backseat to subcommittee meetings on budget, marketing, facilities management, compliance and regulations, human resources, etc. (all good and necessary things, by the way). The idea that brought together a bold, agile, and unified band of brothers and sisters, who operate like Navy Seals and radically live the mission of the idea, morphs into a full-blown organization with multiple layers of direct reports, who need management and oversight. Once this happens, leaders must intentionally create space to innovate, or the organization will eventually fall flat.

Steve Jobs famously said, "It's better to be a pirate than join the navy." He believed it so much that he raised a pirate flag in front of Apple's headquarters. Jobs' point was that a pirate ship is not bogged down with the bureaucracy and politics that prevent the spirit of discovery and disruptive innovation. Jobs was a master at intentionally creating space for his company to innovate, despite Apple having tens of thousands of employees and a massive org chart. He made innovation the cornerstone of Apple's mission, vision, and culture.

One of the greatest challenges to the long-term viability of a successful company is the ability to continually innovate and iterate its products, creating new products for emerging markets. In the tech space, there are two types of companies: those that disrupt and those that get disrupted. It's interesting that some disrupted companies like AOL and Yahoo were once the disruptors (as the preeminent pioneers of email, internet, and search engines in the early days of mass web adoption). But they stayed in their lane, stopped creating new products and no longer expanded into developing markets.

Where would Amazon be if it never expanded beyond an online book store? What if Google was only a search engine? They would have fallen down the path of Yahoo and AOL, and some other upstart innovative tech company would have picked up where they left off. This, in some ways, was the plight of Xerox, which is still viable in its lane (in large part due to Starkweather's laser printer), but nowhere near Apple in terms of valuation and influence.

Starkweather could have easily fallen in line with the status quo and let go of his idea of a laser printer. He could have listened to his boss, and probably still had a successful career at Xerox, which was already considered a highly innovative company at that time.

But Starkweather was a chaos pilot, pursuing and materializing an impossible idea for the good of humanity. Inevitably, moonshot-takers will operate in an intense and (sometimes) prolonged amount of chaos because they are creating a new facet to the way society operates. A new path is just a wild frontier until it is forged.

The good news is that Holy Spirit-led innovators like Starkweather have a secret weapon to overcome the chaos. It is the Kingdom of Heaven, Jesus, residing in their hearts and directing their steps.

Jesus is the ultimate chaos pilot. All heaven and earth submit to His authority. In Him all things exist, are sustained, and find order.

We see this in the story of Jesus calming the storm that the disciples were convinced would end their lives. They woke Jesus from His nap, crying out for Him to do something, and He said to the sea, "Peace, be still." And the wind and sea obeyed because they recognized the Word of God, Jesus, through Whom all things were made.

In the beginning, God created the heavens and the earth. The earth was without form, in a state of chaos. Darkness was everywhere, and God said, "Let there be light," separating night and day. God used light to bring order to the chaos. (Genesis 1:1-4 NKJV)

"In the beginning was the Word (Jesus), and the Word was with God, and the Word was God. He was in the beginning with God. All things were made through Him, and without Him nothing was made that was made. In Him was life, and the life was the *light* of men. And the light shines in the darkness, and the darkness did not comprehend it." (John 1:1-5 NKJV, emphasis added).

Jesus is the light that brings order to chaos, and His light emanates from our entanglement with Him. We can walk into any situation, no matter how new and unfamiliar it is, and have confidence knowing that we are the calm in the storm. We represent the path waiting to be forged from heaven to earth.

6. Renew your mind

As believers, we are called to consistently renew our minds, not falling into the patterns of world-thinking, so that we can always reveal and validate the good, acceptable and perfect will of God from glory to glory. (Romans 12:2)

When God speaks, He creates. Of course, there are absolutes in God's nature. He is the Creator of the world and the Author of life. He is our healer. He is our peace. He is our protector and provider. He is good, generous, loving, faithful, all-knowing and all-powerful, gracious, and an ever-present help in a time of need.

But God is not confined to a template. This is evident in the many different ways Jesus healed in scripture.

When the centurion came to Jesus and asked him to heal his servant, Jesus said, "Go your way; and as you have believed, so let it be done for you." And the servant was healed that same hour. (Matthew 8:13)

When Peter's mother in-law was sick to the point of near death, Jesus came to her, stood over her and rebuked the fever, and the sickness left (Luke 4:38-40).

Jesus healed the deaf-mute of Decapolis by pulling him away from the crowds, putting His finger in the man's ear, spitting and touching his tongue, and commanding the man's hearing and speaking to be opened. Immediately the man was healed, and Jesus told the crowd not to tell anyone. But they couldn't help proclaim the goodness and miracle-working power of Jesus (Mark 7:31-37).

When Jesus healed the demon-possessed man in Gadarenes, he told him to go home and tell his friends what great things the Lord had done for him, and how He had compassion for him (Mark 5:1-20).

When Jesus healed the blind man at Bethsaida, He took him away from the crowd, spit on his eyes, laid His hands on him, and asked the man if He saw anything. The man said he saw men like trees walking. Jesus put His hands on his eyes again, and the man's vision was completely restored. Jesus then told him not to tell anyone in town what had happened (Mark 8:22-26).

When Jesus encountered Bartimaeus the blind beggar in Jericho, He didn't lay hands on him. Rather, he asked Bartimaeus what he wanted Him to do. To which Bartimaeus replied, "My Master, please let me see again." Jesus responded, "Your faith heals you. Go in peace, with your sight restored." And, instantly the man was healed (Mark 10:51-52).

When Jesus saw a woman, who was crippled and hunched over for 18 years, He called her over to Him, laid His hands on her and healed her of her infirmity (Luke 13:10-14).

As Jesus was on His way to heal Jairus's daughter, who was sick to the point of near death, a woman who had suffered from continual bleeding for 12 years pushed through crowds to touch His prayer shawl, and she was healed (Mark 5:21-43).

To some, Jesus laid hands on and they were healed. To others He spoke the word healing, and they were healed.

To some, He told not to share what He had done. To others, He instructed them to proclaim the miracle they had received from Him to everyone.

To some, He saw and initiated healing. To others, they sought Him out and initiated the healing through their faith.

The one constant, however, through all of Jesus's miracles is that He is the complete fullness of our good and loving Father in human form (2 Corinthians 9). In the examples I just shared, the common denominator is Jehovah Rapha (Jesus is Healer). Our faith in His goodness and love is an invitation for Jesus to supplant anything contrary to God's will with the superior reality of the Kingdom of Heaven, in Whom there is no sickness, death, disease, oppression or any form of evil.

One of the most common mistakes among believers is when we try to create a formula around how God has moved in the past. God wants to move in relationship with us, and has individualized solutions for us and through us. The moment we confine what God can do to how He's moved in the past, we risk shifting our focus from His presence to a process or methodology.

Let me be clear: this is not license to do whatever we think is good, and then slap a God-label on it. What God says to you will always align with who the Word of God says He is. He will never ask you to sin, coerce others for your own selfish-ambition, hurt yourself, or spend time away from Him. But when we continually renew our mind by spending time with our Father, more and more we see how He sees, and respond to what He is saying to us in the current season.

When we launched Bethel Tech, one of the concerns among some people in the Bethel environment was that the online modality for our revival group (the spiritual formation course of our program) would not create the same fruit as an in-person revival group. I get the concern, and there is something unique and special about interacting with each other in person.

However, there is also something special about being able to connect with people all over the globe, who are not able to drop everything and move to Redding, CA for an in-person program. God is not confined to the limits of geography, and the power of His Holy Spirit can and does reach through the computer screen to heal sickness and disease, set people free from oppression, restore relationships, and connect the Body of Christ.

Bethel Tech's revival group was a proof of concept that unlocked a new opportunity for Bethel, including the launch of Bethel School of Supernatural Ministry's online modality. As a result, BSSM Online has become a powerful platform for the miracle-working power of God and has expanded BSSM's reach as an apostolic training center.

Additionally, what God was doing with Bethel Tech in our first two years of operation gave our team the necessary knowledge and experience to help other parts of Bethel build strong community, connection and accountability in an online channel. This was especially important during Covid-19, when our schools and church couldn't meet in person for over a year.

God is the same yesterday, today and forever (Hebrews

13:8), but He also has a history of using new wineskin for a fresh outpouring of His glory and goodness so that all would encounter His love with the right word in the right season (Mark 2:22). When we continually renew our minds in alignment with what God is saying right now, we create space to innovate with God to materialize heavenly solutions for earthly problems.

7. Imagine with God

Jesus is able to do exceedingly abundantly above all that we ask, think, or imagine, according to the power that works in us (Ephesians 3:20). And just like Jesus, we are called to bring into right-standing any area that is contrary to the superior reality of the kingdom of heaven. Imagine what it would look like if instead of only focusing on how many people show up to our Sunday church services, we were focused on bringing the Church to people, using every technology and communication channel possible. What if, as Spirit-led innovators, we partnered with God to create new technologies to bring His goodness to all the ends of the earth?

Recently, the YouVersion Bible app just surpassed 500 million downloads, and it is one of the top downloaded apps in the history of the Apple app store. The idea stemmed from Founder Bobby Gruenewald's desire to have an easier way to read His Bible than carrying a physical Bible everywhere. From that simple desire to draw closer to the Father through His Word, Bobby, along with co-founder and COO Terry Storch, in partnership with Craig Groeschel's Life Church in Edmond, Oklahoma, came up with a moonshot idea that would create a way for anyone with internet access to read the Bible.

In its first iteration as a website, YouVersion nearly failed because it wasn't mobile-friendly. At the time, Apple had just released the iPhone, which became an instant cultural hit and technology disruptor. Seemingly overnight, people were shifting their online viewing habits from laptops and personal computers to their smartphones.

Seeing where the market was going, Bobby and Terry pivoted YouVersion to become the first and only Bible app in the rollout of the Apple app store in 2008. To date, the YouVersion Bible app has been translated into 1,750 languages, and even has access into some countries that won't allow physical Bibles.

What I love about the YouVersion story is that, like me, neither Bobby nor Terry are software developers. They simply had an idea to bring the gospel of Jesus to everyone everywhere so that all would have an opportunity to encounter the goodness of God through His Word. God ordered their steps, bringing the right people around them to make it a reality. Today, YouVersion's control center is a technological and operational marvel, with a team of software developers, UIUX designers and data scientists creating new products to spread the gospel and analyzing the application's impact on users across the globe.

God will open doors that no man can shut when you think big with Him. His desires become your desires, and He is faithful to fulfill the desires of your heart.

YouVersion's "why" for technology moved humanity heavenward, wildly pursuing a seemingly impossible goal to bring the Word of God to all the nations. And they're doing it! In addition to multiple versions of the Bible readily available at the push of a mobile icon, YouVersion now has content, devotionals and specific prayers to help people in every season of their lives.

"I have heard numerous stories that have been reported about how the YouVersion app has helped people overcome severe depression, suicidal thoughts or saved their lives or restored their broken marriages and relationships," Gruenewald shared in an interview with *The Christian Post.* "God spoke to them through the app. Their eternity is changed. And it's not the app, it's the Bible that is transformative."[102]

In addition to imagining with God, Bobby and Terry, got themselves out of the lab early to be the light of Jesus, they embraced ~~failure~~ learning by building a mobile app and navigating that season's chaos of disruption with the rise of the iPhone. But above all else, they treasured what God treasures, bringing good news to the poor, freedom to the brokenhearted, new eyes for the blind to see, liberty to the captives, and making disciples of all nations.

8. Don't despise the small beginnings

The Lord tells us not to despise the small beginnings (Zechariah 4:10). He takes delight in the work getting started.

People often ask me how I built Bethel Tech's business plan, and I tell them the only good part of Bethel Tech's business plan was that I did it, moving the idea from concept to reality. It was a clunky plan, to say the least, and I would do it much differently now; but it did show the passion behind the mission and vision, along with a glimpse of a strategy to launch and grow.

And most importantly, God told me to do it. No doubt it could have been tweaked a thousand times, but then we'd still be waiting to launch the school to this day.

I believe faith is spelled "t-r-u-s-t." When we trust what the Lord is saying, we have full confidence to go and do what He is asking us to do, knowing that He is with us and faithful to fulfill His promises (Psalm 145:13). We just have to partner with Him to manifest solutions from the invisible realm into the material world.

Astro Teller, CEO of Google X, said it well:

> The prevailing culture is one of deep analysis and careful modeling of downsides. You can't pre-business-plan a moonshot any more than you can paint a masterpiece via color-by-numbers given to you by a committee. It's no surprise that our creative muscles have atrophied.[103]

Teller and his Google X team would rephrase "don't despise the small beginnings" as "learning to love v0.crap":

> Years of schooling and corporate conditioning have taught us that it's bad to hand in less-than-polished work. But when you're taking moonshots, it's nearly impossible to get things right the first time. Or even the second or third time. Rather than waste time trying to perfect something right off the bat, learn to love what we call "version 0.crap" — the earliest, scrappiest version of your work that you can get honest, open feedback on. This first prototype will help you quickly understand how your ideas

can be refined and what experiments you should run to keep iterating on them.

At Bethel Tech, we have a vision and mission to impact hundreds of thousands of people across the globe by providing a fast and affordable training pathway to learn in-demand skills for high-paying, high-growth careers in Tech. We believe true transformation starts with knowing one's identity in Christ. And the combination of Kingdom values and in-demand tech training is a powerful force that will unlock revival to and through the tech space. I see it in my heart and mind on a daily basis, and often in my dreams at night.

But we had a very humble start. As a non-profit subsidiary of a church, we bootstrapped everything. Bootstrapping a start-up means we had no assets and didn't raise capital through angel investors or venture capital firms. Bethel blessed us with a start-up loan, which in the church world was large, but in the coding bootcamp world was small. We had to be resourceful and faithful stewards with what we had, and that meant private-labeling, or outsourcing, areas of our school that I would have preferred to build in-house from the start.

When we announced our program at the Bethel Leaders Advance Conference in November 2017, we had hundreds of people curious about what we were doing, but they had no real interest in attending our school. Most of them were just curious to see what Bethel was up to. We launched our first cohort in January 2018 with 20 students, and had 120 students in our first year.

I like to think big, and my expectation was that we would

have at least 3x that number in our first year, but God reminded me that small beginnings are a great foundation for a big dream. Bethel Tech's humble beginning afforded us the opportunity to iterate without causing a lot of headaches for a large student population. Because of our small enrollment, we were able to better connect with our early-adopter students to discover what was working and what needed to be tweaked.

Those students are just as much pioneers for Bethel Tech as our team is, and they have become part of our Bethel Tech family with whom we still stay close years later. It has been amazing to see up close and personal how God has honored their faithfulness and pioneering spirit to enroll in an unproven program. Many of them are working for major companies and have been promoted multiple times.

As we've proven our concept, we've been able to build and take ownership of the parts of our business we had to private-label at the beginning. Also, doors are opening to new opportunities for us to use our program, like helping developing countries and underserved communities, that we wouldn't have been able to steward effectively when we launched.

We've always said we don't want to be the best coding bootcamp in the world; we want to be the best *for* the world. I'm happy to say that five years into our school, I believe we offer the highest level of service and support in the online higher education space. We are adding new programs, and our students are thriving mentally, spiritually, physically and emotionally.

Our students are also getting great jobs, which is a key objective of our program. Combined with an excellent curriculum and a beautiful culture of community fostered through our revival groups, I can confidently say we are becoming the best bootcamp *for* the world.

The dream is becoming a reality, and I believe we've only scratched the surface of what God wants to do with us. I believe our students will create new technologies that bring humanity heavenward. I believe our students are the next generation of tech leadership that embody the excellence of Christ in both skill and character. I believe entire communities in developing countries will be radically transformed because of the integrity-driven tech talent hubs that are created as a result of setting up Bethel Tech sites in their villages, towns and cities. Ultimately, I believe all of this fruit will lead to everyone across the globe experiencing the goodness of God because of our involvement and influence in the tech space.

Our team never loses sight of our small, humble beginning, and we are grateful for it. Humility and gratitude for God's goodness in our lives (individually and as a collective team) are core values that drive us into the next level of what God wants us to do and how He wants to partner with us to move humanity heavenward.

9. Keep the main thing the main thing

In the Sermon on Mount, Jesus tells the crowd of people to "Seek first the Kingdom of God and His righteousness, and all these things shall be added unto you." (Matthew 6:33 NKJV) As Kingdom-minded moonshot-takers, it is imperative that we always keep the main thing the main thing—seeking and responding to the presence of God in close relationship with Him. Everything else falls into place when we make Matthew 6:33 our life's posture.

In His sermon on the mount, Jesus also said, "To enter the narrow gate; for wide is the gate that leads to destruction. Difficult and narrow is the gate which leads to life, and there are few who find it." (Matthew 7:13-14) He later tells His disciples that it is impossible for man alone to enter the gate to eternal life, but with God, all things are possible. Those who take the narrow path are the ones qualified to bring heaven to earth.

If we're not careful, we can easily shift our focus from the main thing to a bunch of the minor things. Soon we find ourselves forgetting our "why," and we fall trap to a religious mindset, valuing systems over our Savior and the sheep He has called us to help. If we prioritize the "all these things" above the Kingdom of God, we shift down to an earth-to-heaven approach, trying to solve earthly problems outside of God.

About a year after Bethel Tech launched, I was in a Bethel leaders meeting with Bill Johnson, sharing an update about our school. By this time our first students had recently graduated from our 9-month program, and they were starting to land jobs. I remember Bill throwing his hands in the air and saying, "Who'd have thunk it!"

It was one of the most wonderful things to hear about our school. Here was the father of our house, who has impacted millions of people across the globe, joyfully surprised at our success. Not that he didn't think it could happen, but the idea of a Christian coding school seemed to come out of nowhere. I liken it to opening gifts on Christmas morning as a kid, and discovering one more hidden present under the tree after you thought all the gifts had been opened.

I have the privilege of sharing Bethel Tech updates with Bill on a regular basis. We mostly talk about the student testimonies and our vision to fuel revival to and through the most influential spheres of society. Bethel Tech would not exist without Bill modeling what it looks like to keep Jesus the main thing. If I had to describe him with one scripture it would be Matthew 6:33. Because of his commitment to seek first the Kingdom of Heaven and His righteousness, a large oak tree of life has grown in the 26 years he and his wife Beni have led Bethel Church. Bethel Tech is a branch that has sprouted on that tree, along with so many of our other areas of impact like Bethel School of Supernatural Ministry (BSSM), Bethel Music, Bethel Media, Bethel Global Response, and Bethel Leaders Network.

I believe we will see an outpouring of Holy Spirit-led moonshot ideas from the Body of Christ when we keep our eyes fixed on Jesus and desire, above everything else, to go deeper in our relationship with Him. Kingdom-minded innovation is the fruit of a personal relationship with God.

There is such an ease to Holy Spirit downloads when we are walking hand-in-hand with our loving Father. Our perspective shifts from reacting to what we think He is saying to simply responding to His voice. Reaction is an outward-in perspective. Response is an inward-outpouring of the heart when our greatest desire is a personal relationship with Jesus.

10. Have an eternity mindset

God is the creator of time. Time is on His side, and therefore on our sides as well.

The ancient Greeks had two words to describe time. The

first was "Chronos" which was a quantitative measurement of time. It's where we get the word "chronological". Their second word for time was "Kairos," which was a qualitative measurement of time. Kairos time was measured by the intersection of favor and opportunity. As believers, we recognize this as the intersection of Divine favor and opportunity.

A season characterized by multiple Kairos moments is an epoch. As we've discussed, the mid-19th century in the time of Maxwell, Faraday and Babbage was an epoch in science that shaped our modern technology and communication networks.

However, these two measurements of time are just subheadings under a larger measurement of time—eternity. What God did with Frideswide. What He did with Maxwell. What He is doing at this moment with us, He is also doing for 10, 20, 100, 1000 years from now and for all eternity.

What if time were a physical dimension, like a large room labeled "eternity" on the front door? And, what if the actions you took now interacted with the actions of Maxwell in the 19th century, Sir Isaac Newton's discovery of gravity in the 17th century, and Johannes Gutenberg's invention in the 15th century, the printing press, which helped spark the Protestant Reformation and Scientific Revolution?

What if, in another part of the eternity room, we walk over to Moses and the parting of the Red Sea or Jesus's Sermon on the Mount or Paul's speech to the Areopagus in Athens? What if we traveled back even further than that to the story of Creation, in which God chose you before the foundation of the world?

If eternity were a room, could it be as simple as walking

through spacetime across the room? The Word of God says we are surrounded by a cloud of witnesses (Hebrews 12:1) right after recounting the incredible faith exploits of the patriarchs and matriarchs of the people of God (Hebrews 11). The legends of our faith heritage– Noah, Abraham and Sarah, Moses, Elijah, David, Esther, Rahab, Daniel, the disciples, Paul– are all part of our story, simultaneously impacting the moment they were in and the moment we are in today.

A couple of years ago, I had a dream in which a group of software developers were in a computer lab programming on their computers. The developers were located in different parts of the world, but they were all together in this one room. There was a teacher walking around the room, peering over their shoulders to see what they were programming. The teacher was Jesus. When He looked at a programmer's work, He would say, "Well done good and faithful servant. Have you thought about doing this?" And when Jesus asked the question, Spirit-led innovation was conceived from an invisible realm into the physical world to move humanity heavenward.

Spirit-led innovators have an acute awareness of their Kingdom heritage and history, and they understand that what they do now shapes eternity. They recognize that, as children of God, our stories are interwoven throughout history. We are a part of God's original moonshot idea to live in intimate relationship with His creation for all eternity.

8

SPIRITUAL INTELLIGENCE

"For 'who has known the mind of the Lord that he may instruct Him?' But we have the mind of Christ."
I Corinthians 2:16 NKJV

I find it fascinating that Maxwell, Faraday, Lord Kelvin, and Babbage attributed their discoveries to an active relationship with God that opened a door into an invisible realm ripe with Divine solutions for the physical world. Their belief in God was not rooted in learned theology, alone; it was shaped by His personal presence in their lives.

It's as though they were thinking with and like God. Or, as the Apostle Paul describes in I Corinthians 2:6-16 (NKJV), they functioned with the mind of Christ:

> However, we speak wisdom among those who are mature, yet not the wisdom of this age, nor of the rulers of this age, who are coming to nothing. But we speak the wisdom of God in a mystery, the hidden wisdom which God ordained before the ages for our glory, which none of the rulers of this age knew; for had they known, they would

not have crucified the Lord of glory.

But as it is written: "Eye has not seen, nor ear heard, nor have entered into the heart of man the things which God has prepared for those who love Him." But God has revealed them to us through His Spirit. For the Spirit searches all things, yes, the deep things of God. For what man knows the things of a man except the spirit of the man which is in him? Even so no one knows the things of God except the Spirit of God.

Now we have received, not the spirit of the world, but the Spirit who is from God, that we might know the things that have been freely given to us by God. These things we also speak, not in words which man's wisdom teaches but which the Holy Spirit teaches, comparing spiritual things with spiritual. But the natural man does not receive the things of the Spirit of God, for they are foolishness to him; nor can he know them, because they are spiritually discerned. But he who is spiritual judges all things, yet he himself is rightly judged by no one.

For who has known the mind of the Lord that he may instruct Him? But we have the mind of Christ.

God reveals His wisdom to us in the Spirit realm to manifest His will on earth as it is in heaven. This spiritual intelligence is incomprehensible to man apart from God, but once manifested in the physical realm, the outward manifestation becomes part of humankind's collective consciousness and serves as a foundation for technological innovation and scientific discovery—even if man doesn't remember or realize its origin.

My mentor and friend, Kris Vallotton, who is the co-founder of Bethel School of Technology and senior associate leader at Bethel church in Redding, CA, wonderfully describes this intellect in the unseen realm as spiritual intelligence (SQ). Look at the following passage from his book *Spiritual Intelligence: The Art of Thinking Like God*:

> You've probably heard about the Intelligent Quotient (IQ) that measures how well someone can use information and logic to answer questions. And, you've probably heard of Emotional Quotient (EQ) that measures one's ability to understand, use, and manage his or her own emotions. But, Spiritual Intelligence (or Spiritual Quotient - SQ) is one's ability to discern, perceive and judge the spiritual dimensions that are at work in and around you, and manage this realm towards a positive outcome. [104]

There exist three heavens. The first heaven is the physical world, which can be perceived and defined by our natural senses– what we can touch, see, smell, hear, and taste.

The second heaven is what we see in Ephesians 6:12, when it says that we don't battle against flesh and blood, but against principalities and the rulers of darkness of this age, against spiritual hosts of wickedness in the heavenly places. The demonic realm exists in the second heaven.

And then, there is a third heaven. This is eternal paradise, from which God expelled Satan and a third of the angels for their rebellion (Revelations 12:9), and of which Paul states he knew a man who was caught up to the third heaven, or paradise, and heard inexpressible words (2 Corinthians 12:2-4).

Jesus, who brought heaven wherever He went because

heaven is who He is, calls us His ambassadors and instructs us to pray for God's Kingdom to come on earth right now (Matthew 6:10). It is our responsibility to unveil solutions from the third heaven to solve first-heaven problems such as poverty, disease, oppression, murder, injustice, and anything else that is contrary to His will.

There is not a first-heaven problem that hasn't already been solved in the third heaven. It is up to us, as containers of God's hope and authority, to partner with Him and manifest those solutions in the physical realm. Failure to do so relinquishes authority to the spiritual hosts of wickedness in the second heaven, which always seek to steal, kill and destroy.

Furthermore, in *Spiritual Intelligence*, Kris talks about the spirit of origin that is referenced in Ephesians 6:12: "Our struggle is not against flesh and blood, but against the rulers, against the powers, against the world forces of this darkness, against the spiritual forces of wickedness in the heavenly places." The word "rulers" in this scripture is the Greek word "arche," which means origin or the underlying, intangible substance of cause.

The Apostle Paul, who wrote the book of Ephesians, identifies a battle against demonic spirits from the second heaven, and specifically calls out a spirit of "origin." The devil can only attempt to pervert or counterfeit truth, and he sets his sights on counterfeiting anything that has power.

The most powerful revelation in the history of humankind is knowing the origin of and purpose for our existence. Our origin points to our Creator and the lengths to which He will go to be with us. When sin entered into our consciousness through the fall of man, our loving Father did not abandon us, even though He is the antithesis of sin.

He sent and sacrificed His blameless son, Jesus, so that we would be restored to our original design of everlasting relationship with our Creator. He who had no sin became sin for us, so that we might become the righteousness of God and live in right-standing with Him (2 Corinthians 5:21). All we have to do is believe and receive the gift of Jesus as our Lord and Savior.

The "arche" spirit in Ephesians is a counterfeit source of origin and dark governor of confusion commissioned by Satan to distort the truth of our existence. The mere fact we exist, as children of God, terrifies the enemy because we have been given authority over him. He will stop at nothing to hide the truth of our origin because a person being what God designed him or her to be is a constant reminder that Satan has lost the war and his fate is already sealed in eternal damnation. But that doesn't mean he won't do anything he can to bring down God's creation with him in flames.

I had heard Kris speak about SQ before he wrote his book. In fact, he had previously shared it at Google's headquarters in Mountainview, CA on a panel discussion Bethel Tech hosted discussing the intersection of faith and technology.

When Kris spoke, he opened by saying he is probably the least technological person in the room. Then, he proceeded to share about the three heavens, having the mind of Christ, tapping into SQ, and revealing third-heaven solutions for first-heaven problems. As he shared, I saw the audience, who were some of the most brilliant Christian technologists in the world, lean into what he was saying. They were literally sitting on the edges of their seats.

The atmosphere shifted in the tech space that day, and that moment was instrumental in opening my heart to receive God's word about redeeming the tech space. One hundred years from now, I believe we will look back at that panel discussion as an anchor point in redeeming the tech space so all would encounter the goodness of God. I would not be writing this book without that moment at Google and Kris's follow-up SQ teachings during our weekly leadership meetings.

At Google, Kris shared a personal experience operating with spiritual intelligence. Prior to entering full-time ministry at Bethel Church, Kris and his wife, Kathy, owned an auto parts store in the early 1990s. As their business grew, they realized they needed an updated payment software system. They spent over $30 thousand for a new system, and had a computer engineer install it. Unfortunately, the software only offered three payment tiers, and their business needed five tiers.

Thinking this would be a quick fix, Kris and Kathy asked the engineer to make an adjustment to the software. He couldn't, and his recommendation was to buy a new system that would cost over $50 thousand.

In the natural, Kris and Kathy were in an impossible situation. Except, like the story of Frideswide, with God all things are possible.

Kris prayed to God, and he was confident that He would provide a solution. One night, while Kris and Kathy were sleeping, the Lord gave Kris lines of numbers, letters and characters in a dream. Kris woke up and immediately wrote the lines down on a notepad. He then woke Kathy up, and told her he thought these lines were the solution for their software problem.

Around 4 a.m., Kris and Kathy drove to the auto parts store. Kathy turned on the computer and typed the lines into the system. Immediately, the screen turned green and Kathy realized they were in the backend of the computer. The lines God gave Kris were lines of code! Kris had no idea about coding, and yet there they were in the back of the computer, making adjustments to the payment software system. Lo and behold they were able to add two additional payment tiers, saving themselves thousands of dollars!*

Here's what I love most about Kris and Kathy's SQ story: God showed up as an ever-present help in a time of need for the Vallottons. But, what He was doing to them in that moment over 30 years ago, He was simultaneously doing to and through them right now. That loving, personal moment with Jesus sparked a journey in which Kris became acutely aware of spiritual intelligence.

I believe we are on the cusp of a new season in which the greatest intellect will come from faith in God and SQ. At its core, Bethel Tech is an SQ institute.

Not long after the Google event, Bethel Tech Director of Spiritual Instruction, Richard Gordon, who has become one of my best friends, shared with me how God gave him an algorithm in a dream that became the foundation for his Master's in Cryptography thesis while attending university in South Africa. The algorithm not only helped him with his thesis; it was published in textbooks that are used to this day.

---

* Fun footnote: "lo" was the first internet transmission sent from UCLA to Stanford in 1969. The full word UCLA researchers tried to send was "login", but the transmission crashed after the first two letters. Lo and behold the internet was born.

The success of his thesis propelled him into a successful career in the tech space, and his experience tapping into SQ has become a building block upon which we teach our students.

When I think of the intersection of faith and technology, I immediately see Richard Gordon's face and his awesome dreadlocks. And now, I also see the thousand-plus Bethel Tech students entering the tech space whom he's discipled.

Adib Hanna

Adib Hanna is a dear friend, who led instruction for Bethel Tech for over two years. His Jesus testimony is so radical it deserves its own book, but I'll share with you an overview of his story, which includes a heavenly download he received in a dream that changed the course of his life.

Before Adib got saved, he was heavily involved in witchcraft. Growing up in Lebanon, Adib and his group of witches and warlocks were famous in their village for their dark magic. They were known to cast spells, stand in fire unscathed, levitate, and climb walls. But God pursued Adib.

Adib loved music and ended up playing bass for a heavy metal Christian rock group. The lead singer would later tell Adib, he was concerned he was a Satanist, but God specifically told him to add Adib to the band.

The band would take Bethel Music songs, and turn them into heavy metal covers. Just imagine "Ever Be" or "You Make Me Brave" with a Metallica makeover. I mean, if I had a dime for every story I've heard that started with "So a Satanist was playing bass in a Christian metal rock band that covered Bethel Music songs," I'd be a dime short of ten cents.

His bandmates would share Bible stories with Adib, and the lyrics of the songs were softening his heart. Then, at a concert, a young woman in the audience shared the gospel with him. For every one of his questions or rebuttals to the gospel, the woman had an answer based on scripture.

Adib is a genius. His IQ is through the roof, and he even received a college scholarship to play chess. It is nearly impossible to out-intellect him, and here was this person meeting and exceeding his level, using scripture and Divine wisdom to do it.

On top of that, Adib's bandmates became his good friends. They loved him and lived their lives representing the love of Jesus in authenticity. They also prayed for him consistently.

The combination of his bandmates and the woman from the audience, whom he befriended, led Adib to an encounter with the Lord. Talk about a Divine set-up.

One night, Jesus visited Adib in a dream. He awoke and gave his life to Jesus. The next morning, he couldn't stop smiling and everything he saw was illuminated with a bright light. When he walked, it was like his feet were barely touching the ground.

He was freaked out. So, to stop it, Adib tried to drop an f-bomb, but he physically couldn't. He said it was like his spirit wouldn't let him. Adib found incomprehensible joy in receiving Christ, and like the Apostle Paul's conversion experience on the road to Damascus, he went all in.

Immersing himself in the Bible and reading books by Bill Johnson on the power of the Holy Spirit, Adib went throughout his village and other towns in Lebanon laying his hands on people and healing them in the name of Jesus. The same hands that used to curse people and cast spells were now manifesting heaven's superior reality on earth.

On a mission to learn more about Bethel Church, he found out about Bethel School of Supernatural Ministry (BSSM), and came to Redding for the first-year BSSM program in 2016 on a student visa. In the summer between his first and second year at BSSM, while back in Lebanon, Adib had another dream. In it, he was teaching students at Bethel how to code and partner with the Holy Spirit to create tech solutions. This was the summer of 2017, around the same time my family and I moved to Redding, CA to start Bethel Tech.

We officially announced Bethel Tech at a Bethel Leaders Conference in November 2017. When Adib found out, he made a beeline for me.

Adib is a very determined individual. When he puts his mind to something, it is as good as done.

He introduced himself and immediately shared his dream with me. I didn't have a place for him, and quite honestly, didn't know what to do with him. This guy was either going to be a partner in destiny, or I was going to have to get a restraining order. There didn't seem to be any middle ground.

Adib and I met again, this time over coffee. Quickly, I could see that he was a brilliant developer, who was on fire for Jesus and had a heart of gold. He wanted to help us in any way possible. He started by overhauling and maintaining our website, and then he volunteered to mentor our students when we launched our first cohort in early 2018.

When we looked at the results of our initial student feedback surveys, overwhelmingly our students shared their two favorite parts of our program were revival groups with Richard Gordon and mentor sessions with Adib Hanna.

Six months later, we hired Adib as our lead instructor, and our young school went from good to great. Adib would find his future wife in Redding, and they just had their first child. The Lord has blessed him financially with multiple streams of income, and he has been able to support his parents and siblings, who recently had to flee Lebanon because of the country's economic crash and social unrest.

He has impacted hundreds of students' lives, who are now excelling in the tech space, and he is collaborating with some of the leading developers in the tech space to create emerging technologies, specifically in the area of blockchain.

Jesus visited Adib in dreams. His life has been forever impacted, and he is impacting the lives of others because he listened, trusted, and obeyed what God was asking him to do. Adib's spiritual intelligence was a key to innovating with God to move humanity heavenward.

On the topic of dreams, it is fascinating how many innovators in the world of science have received downloads while they're sleeping or in visions that have changed the course of history. Below are just a few notable examples.

Russian chemist, Dmitri Mendeleev, created the periodic table in 1867 from a vision while he was asleep. "In a dream I saw a table where all the elements fell into place as required," Mendeleev said. "Awakening, I immediately wrote it down on a piece of paper."[105]

Danish physicist, Niehls Bohr, who was also a pioneer in quantum theory, developed the atomic model in 1913 based on a dream he had in which he was sitting on the sun with planets "hissing around on tiny chords."[106] Bohr's model explained why atoms emit light of fixed wavelengths, which served as a building block for quantum mechanics. He received the Nobel Prize in Physics in 1922, and he helped refugees escape Nazi Germany during World War II.

Albert Einstein had a dream as a teenager that led him to pursue a career in science and became the basis for his theory of relativity. In it he was sledding down a hill with his friends at night. As he continued to accelerate, Einstein realized he was nearing the speed of light.

As he looked up and saw the stars, he noticed they were being refracted into colors he had never seen before. "I was filled with a sense of awe," Einstein described. "I understood in some way that I was looking at the most important meaning in my life."[107] Einstein would later say his entire scientific career had been a meditation on that one dream as a teenager.

Danny Kim

A year after the Google panel discussion, I heard Danny Kim, founder and Chief Technology Officer (CTO) of the cybersecurity company, Full Armor, share an incredible SQ story at the Silicon Valley Prayer Breakfast. Shortly after Danny and his partners launched Full Armor in the mid-1990s, they landed the whale of all client accounts– Walmart. Full Armor was responsible for keeping Walmart's cashier software secure. When Danny received the first check from Walmart, he was elated to cash it.

But right after cashing the check, Danny received a phone call from an attorney on Walmart's legal team. Something was wrong with the software code, and the cashier system was down for all of Walmart's stores. They were losing millions of dollars every hour that the system was down. The attorney notified Danny they had stopped payment on the check, and would be suing Full Armor for the issue.

Danny asked the attorney to give Full Armor twenty-four hours to fix the issue, and he obliged. All day, he and his team scoured hundreds of thousands of lines of code, but couldn't find the issue. In the 23rd hour (literally), Danny's team approached him.

"Danny, it's time," they said. He assumed they meant it was time to give up.

But his team had a different idea. "It's time to pray," they added. Desperate, but reinvigorated by his team's hope and resiliency, Danny and his team prayed. As he closed his eyes, he started to see lines of code scroll rapidly on a computer screen in his mind. Then the scroll stopped and highlighted a specific incorrect character on a line of code.

Danny opened his eyes, and knew exactly where the flaw was. He went to the character on the line of code and fixed it! Walmart's executive team was so impressed with Danny and his team's character and grit that they signed Full Armor on as a long-term cybersecurity vendor –a relationship that exists to this day, nearly 30 years later.

John White

In the early 1990s, John White was an engineer at Boeing, working on a team that partnered with NASA to build the International Space Station (ISS). The ISS is a 460-ton laboratory, roughly the size of a football field, orbiting 250 miles above Earth. It's used for scientific research to answer fundamental questions about our universe through deep space exploration.

In the building process of the ISS, John and his team encountered a seemingly unsolvable problem. Through Spiritual Intelligence (SQ), God gave John the solution:

I worked on the International Space Station. We ran into a problem that no one could solve for about two years even with about 20 NASA PhDs trying to help me.

Not solving the problem would mean a significant redesign of the avionic and experiment support data network. It would have cost about $60M to change.

One night, I dreamed of a solution. It involved math I didn't know and I would need to use software I did know. What I dreamed was how the math was coded in the program and how the primary functioning of the program worked. I was somehow able to see a program run.

The next day I consulted a colleague, asking if he could help me with the math. He gave me a couple of books. My boss asked me to meet with him and the team to discuss making the change. I told them I had a dream and would like to postpone the decision a week until I solidified the solution. A week later, I could show other people the solution and how it would work. The following week the NASA PhDs agreed with the approach, but didn't think the program would work like I dreamed.

My boss had confidence in me and gave me a few months to develop the math algorithms in the program. In the end, the solution allowed me to validate the data communication system that allowed the ISS to navigate, send audio and video to Earth and support experiments throughout the ISS.

I've [since] spoken to industry tech symposia with the message to pay close attention to your dreams. I found more people had questions about understanding dreams and getting inspiration than any technology I presented. It was easy to tell them how God speaks to me all the time about my work. My colleagues are challenged with the idea that God would be interested in promoting science and technology.

John partnered with the Holy Spirit to bring a third-heaven solution for a first-heaven problem. With God, John functioned in the realm of the impossible to the degree that it completely baffled the NASA PhD scientists, who were considered the brightest minds in the scientific community.

John partnered with God to manifest a solution for the ISS. I believe the station will serve as a discovery lab to answer those fundamental questions of the universe that scientists are asking, specifically pointing to *the* answer– God spoke the worlds into existence.

All matter is crying out that God is Creator, from the infinitesimal particles of an atom to the vast expanse of the cosmic universe. Through scientific discovery, the invisible attributes set into existence since the creation of the world are becoming clearly seen. They will be understood by the things that are made, even His eternal power and Godhead to the point that it would be complete foolishness to suggest any other explanation for the origin of existence apart from God (Romans 1:20 NKJV). Just as quantum computing needs more Holy Spirit-led Maxwells to fully actualize its purpose, so too does deep space exploration.

For John, the unfathomable solution opened the door to share how God gave him a heavenly download in a dream, which ultimately magnified the goodness and brilliance of our Creator. It not only solved a $60 million problem, it left no room for any other explanation outside of Divine intervention. The solution didn't just move humanity forward; it moved humanity heavenward.

Since launching Bethel Tech, we've had a number of our students receive lines of code, as well as words of knowledge in dreams and visions from the Lord in their schoolwork and their jobs, similar to Kris, Richard, Adib, Danny, and John. A word of knowledge is a Divine word specific to a fact or situation that could not have been known by natural means.

One of our early graduates was preparing for a tech assessment interview for a highly competitive paid-apprenticeship slot at IBM. With his interview on a Monday, he dedicated the weekend to fully focus on preparing for what coding questions they might ask him to solve.

The challenge for preparing for a coding interview is that the questions are notoriously random and difficult to prepare for. I've heard horror stories from seasoned developers with years of experience who bombed junior-level assessments because the company focused on a particular equation that the interviewee had never seen before.

As part of his preparation, our graduate was praying for the Lord to show him where he needed to focus his attention. The Lord directed him to a book on specific coding algorithms, and told him to spend the weekend learning from the book. In his tech assessment interview on that Monday, he was asked to solve an equation that was taken directly from the book God pointed him to over the weekend. He nailed the interview, and got the final slot for the paid-apprenticeship program, which set him on an amazing journey of experiencing God's goodness. After his apprenticeship at IBM, one of the largest tech companies in the world, he was able to continue to learn and grow his skill on the job, and then landed a six-figure salary at another company.

Plus, he met his future wife, who worked with IBM and helped us build our User Interface/User Experience Design (UIUX) program at Bethel Tech. Talk about glory to glory!

Another one of our early graduates was deciding whether or not he should attend our school or another more established coding bootcamp. And rightfully so. At that point, we were just a few months old, and didn't yet have graduation and job-hire outcomes to validate the quality of our school.

The student received a vision about our school in a dream from the Lord. In the dream, he put in a giant contact lens that was much larger than his eye. When he awoke he heard the Lord say that he needed to expand his vision beyond his own eyesight, and trust the much larger vision the Lord had for his life. He knew that meant stepping out in faith and enrolling in Bethel Tech.

Upon graduation, the student landed a highly-competitive paid internship at YouVersion, beating out graduates at some of the leading universities. After his internship, he got hired as a software developer at Dell, which is one of the largest computer manufacturers in the world.

Another one of our grads was going through a tech assessment interview, and the Lord gave him answers to the questions on the spot. When he solved the problems on the whiteboard and looked at the hiring managers for feedback, he noticed bewildered expressions on their faces. He asked if there was something wrong with his answers. They replied that his answers were correct, but they couldn't figure out how he solved the problems so quickly. A test that typically took an hour to complete took our graduate 30 minutes.

They offered the job to him for around $70 thousand. However, God told him not to take it. The graduate ended up taking another job offer shortly after for $142 thousand! I believe the Lord was teaching our student to trust His voice above everything else, and believe that He had a plan to prosper him and give him a hope and a future, as God declares in Jeremiah 29:11.

Through spiritual intelligence, we not only have access to the mind of Christ; we get to partner with Him to manifest third-heaven solutions for first-heaven problems. The solutions have an exponential and eternal effect for ourselves and for the people who encounter the solution— now and for generations to come.

Above all else, SQ solutions are so radical and incomprehensible, they can only be rationally explained as works from the hands of God. They become an invitation to enlighten the eyes of understanding for the world to see and accept God as Creator and Jesus as Lord and Savior.

9

YADA RELATIONSHIP

"In all your ways acknowledge Him, and He shall direct your paths." Proverbs 3:6 NKJV

So is spiritual intelligence earned through study and application? Immersing oneself in the Word is certainly part of it, because the Bible is an open-door invitation to encounter God; and it allows Him to transform us into His likeness. But study and application for the purpose of knowledge alone defeats the very purpose of God's Word. The Pharisees were experts in the Law, and yet they could not recognize the Kingdom of Heaven as He stood before their very own eyes. They were seeing through counterfeit eyes, as Satan deceived Adam and Eve into using, instead of eyes of understanding of which Paul spoke in Ephesians.

Thinking like and with Jesus is first and foremost rooted in a personal relationship with Him, from which we respond to His presence. We cannot see that which cannot be seen unless we have a close relationship with Jesus, who is the Word.

God's Word is an invitation to a communion relationship with our loving Father. Proverbs 3:5-6 says, "Trust the Lord with all your heart, and lean not on your own understanding. In all your ways acknowledge Him, and He shall direct your paths." The word "acknowledge" in verse 6 is the Hebrew word "yada," which means the most intimate form of knowing. It's the same word we find in Genesis 4:1 where Adam "knew" Eve and they conceived a child.

This passage of scripture has become a foundation in my life, and I'd like to share with you the journey of my "yada" story with Jesus. In it, I hope you will see my SQ is the direct manifestation of an intimate relationship with God. And my moonshot—to bring the goodness of God to all through the tech space—was conceived from listening, trusting and obeying God's voice.

When I share with people that I'm the CEO of Bethel School of Technology, a Christian online coding bootcamp, the inevitable next question is always "Why?" followed up with "How?" Then, the conversation usually shifts to the irony of blending Christian values and tech training. Because, after all, the drive-by narrative regarding the tech space is that it's anti-Christ.

The truth is I didn't grow up thinking that I would be involved in tech in any capacity. My background is in sports journalism, and I grew up aspiring to be the next Bob Costas.

But one core value has always resonated in my heart: I love helping people. I believe that God, the Creator, embedded that value into everyone's DNA because that is who He is, Jehovah-Ezer (Lord, He is our Help), and He made us in His image.

My employment in the world of online higher education

was not out of passion, but necessity. In 2006, a year into our marriage, my wife and I moved from Columbia, MO to Dallas, TX. In Columbia, I was working full-time as a master control operator at the ABC affiliate in mid-Missouri and part-time as a sportswriter at the *Columbia Tribune*. My wife was working as a nanny for a child with special needs, and we felt the Lord call us to Dallas.

By the favor of God, I secured a freelance gig to write sports articles for American Airlines' in-flight magazine, *American Way*. I joke that I went from interviewing the softball coach at the local high school in mid-Missouri to all-star professional athletes.

It's funny how people think that sportswriting is a glamorous job. The reality is it's a hustle with a very low floor. I would write a two thousand-word article every few months and make a couple of thousand dollars, but that certainly wasn't enough to sustain us financially. My steady source of income came from working construction. I remember interviewing the commissioner of the NHL over the phone in an apartment garage I had just swept.

That was an incredibly challenging season in my life because I complicated the goodness of God. The writing gig at *American Way* had the potential to catapult me into a successful career in sports journalism, and I didn't know how to handle it. The truth is I had no idea about my identity in Christ. I thought I alone was responsible for everything in my life, and I had a habit of sabotaging the good things in my life because I didn't consider myself worthy.

There's an old adage that says you will move toward the things you look at. Like, when you're driving and your eyes veer to the right to see something on the side of the road. If you stare in that direction too long, you'll find yourself steering the car in that direction.

Well, I had my eyes fixed on road kill on the side of the road. The road kill was my low self-worth, and it was destroying every good thing in my life, including my marriage.

I was a shell of who I was supposed to be. In my mind, I was a fraud just waiting to be exposed for talking a big game, but not backing it up. The joy of getting a national writing gig was quickly overshadowed by the fear of being completely unqualified to deliver.

Trying to write when you think you can't is torture, and I was torturing myself on a daily basis. I couldn't write, and then I would freak out that I couldn't write. And then I would freak out that I freaked out. In short, I was a freaking mess.

I should have been thankful and motivated by an incredible opportunity to jump from a part-time writer at a small market newspaper to writing articles for a national publication. Instead, I was terrified.

When we don't know who we are in Christ, we don't know how to receive gifts because we do not truly see ourselves as worthy of receiving gifts beyond our own merit. My identity was not connected to who God said I was, but rather a pattern of mimicking the path of those I aspired to be like.

It all culminated with a panic attack in a hotel room in Chicago. Briana and I were on a trip to celebrate her sister's wedding engagement. I had asked for a deadline extension for a story, and I had 48 hours to get it done. This came on the heels of my editor emailing me with the worst subject line imaginable after my first draft: "Rewrite," which is code for "trash everything and start over." I must have stayed up three days straight trying to write a two thousand-word article. The more I tried, the worse it got.

I remember standing in a clothing store in Chicago, and my knees buckling. I caught myself, and I figured I had just been standing too long. That night at the hotel, my body went cold, my vision got blurry, and I started to shake. I was physically, emotionally and mentally exhausted.

I eventually finished the story, and couldn't force myself to read it for months. It wasn't my voice in that story. It was a counterfeit version; someone trying to be like anyone but himself.

I wrote a couple more articles, but realized that I needed a job with a steady income that didn't require me to set my own path. I felt that I didn't have what it took to travel the entrepreneurial path of a freelance writer. At that point in my life, I just needed someone to tell me what to do and what I would get paid if I hit my goals.

A good friend of mine from church asked if I needed a full-time job. He was working for the University of Phoenix as a business development specialist, and he was being promoted to a manager position. At that time, University of Phoenix, and in particular its Dallas campus, was exploding with success. My wife and I wanted to buy a home and start having kids, so I interviewed and accepted a job as a business development specialist, working with local employers to help their employees go back to school.

It was a sales job, which was ironic because I hated sales. A couple of years prior, right after Briana and I got married, I took a job as a used car salesman at a Toyota dealership. I lasted a whole two weeks, never actually making it out of training and onto the sales floor. I hated the manipulative tactics I was being taught. I quit the job, vowing never to work in a sales role again.

And yet, here I was selling online education with a monthly quota of enrollments. But something happened at the University of Phoenix. That innate desire to help people was re-awakened. I would set up a table at an AT&T call center or a Walmart break room and spend time listening to other people's hopes and dreams. I'd sit down with a single mom, who was working multiple jobs just to put food on the table for her kids, and I was moved with compassion to help her in any way I could as she shared her personal and professional goals with me. I was moved with compassion for a twenty-year-old man who set out to be the first person in his family to graduate college, but had to put his degree on hold to help support his parents and siblings.

I became part of their journeys and stories, and I would look for strategic ways to work with their employers to help them pay for tuition. I realized that education was one of the most powerful channels of economic mobility in the world. I wasn't selling to make a quota. I was changing lives.

It was compassion in action, and it ignited a fire inside of me to help as many people as possible. I would set up partnerships with companies, providing tuition discounts and maximizing their employee tuition reimbursement benefits. Over time, I became a trusted education solutions advisor, and companies started asking me for my input on their talent development initiatives.

I didn't consider myself a salesperson, nor have I ever. Instead, I considered it an honor and privilege to help people achieve their personal and professional goals through the power of education.

I was excelling at work, and our first child was on the way. But, I still was operating out of a false sense of identity. I knew Jesus as my savior, but "Lord"? That was a different story. In my mind, I was the lord of my life; and subsequently, I clung to a performance-driven identity.

We closed on our first home, and had some credit card debt. With a kid and mortgage on the way, I felt like we needed a quick infusion of money to get us on the right track financially.

It was 2008, and a friend of mine was making 30 percent returns on short-term real estate investments. I'd watch as he would cash another check, and it looked like the perfect opportunity to make some quick money and pay off what little debt we had.

The only problem was we didn't have the cash to finance the investment, so we took out more debt - $40 thousand worth of debt, to be exact. My wife didn't feel right about it, but we had seen our friends make money off the investment, so we felt like it was worth the risk. We also grew up in a culture that pushed the notion of a wife backing a husband's decisions, no matter how asinine those decisions were. So, against her better judgment, Briana agreed to move forward with the investment.

Quick marriage tip: if you've prayed about a decision and one spouse is not on board with moving forward with it, the answer is "no." Another marriage tip specifically for the husbands: A Holy Spirit-led wife has a unique God-given intuition. Hence the phrase, "a woman's intuition." Celebrate and lean into it!

I could have told you a hundred times over that "get rich

quick" plus "too good to be true" equals a recipe for disaster. But maybe, just maybe this time, it would work for me. After all, I had good intentions. I wasn't trying to buy a Ferrari, I just wanted to provide for my family.

I remember wiring the money to the real estate investment company. This should have been exciting, but everything felt off. I still remember the ominous buzzing sound of the cold blue fluorescent lighting in the conference room at the bank. The sound seemed unusually loud, almost like it was warning me of the imminent danger ahead.

But I pressed on. I convinced myself that the most successful people all took risks. While true, I missed one little detail. Successful people take risks in areas they have at least a general understanding. I knew very little about real estate, less about investing, and even less about finances at that point.

Well, as it turns out, 2008 ended up being a pretty crappy year for the housing market. In fact, 2008 was the year the housing bubble burst and plunged the U.S. economy into a recession. It felt like wiring that money was the tipping point for the entire recession. Of course, it wasn't; but I kid you not, the next day after wiring the money I started reading reports of a housing market crisis that was about to snowball out of control.

"That can't be good," I thought to myself, but the investment was short-term and we were set to get a $12 thousand return in 90 days. Three months went by, and nothing. Then another month and another...crickets.

Our minimum payments for the debt we took on to finance the investment were caving in on us. I connected with the head of the real estate company, and he promised we would see our money soon. We did get about $12k of it back from him, but a month later, we received a letter from the U.S. Department of Justice that said the company was being investigated for fraud. Long story short, we invested in a Ponzi scheme and were on the verge of losing everything.

I was spiraling. I was a failure. I failed my wife, my newborn daughter, myself, God, everyone. I had conditioned myself to find my worth in my accomplishments. Now, in my mind, I was completely worthless.

There were so many nights my wife and I would just cry, as we couldn't pay credit card bills, insurance or the mortgage. We were so close to filing bankruptcy, and actually met with a bankruptcy attorney. Sitting there listening to the attorney give every valid reason why we should file Chapter 13, we both felt in our hearts that it wasn't the right thing to do. I believe bankruptcy can be the right path for people, but it wasn't for us.

God was speaking the same thing to each of us individually and, for the first time, I can remember we both leaned in and shared what God was saying to our hearts and the words were in complete alignment. To be clear, my wife had been doing this since I met her, and it was her listening to God's voice, being in communion relationship with Him, that kept us from falling apart in the early years of our marriage.

But for the first time, in the car driving back from the attorney's office, it felt like Briana and I were doing life together in partnership with God. We determined that God would get us out of our mess. I was bound and determined to do what He said instead of what I thought.

On the work front, I was doing well, and a job opportunity with Kaplan University came along that was $25 thousand more than I was making. It was a great move and increase in pay; but we were still in the red every month, and we were months behind on our mortgage. I got second jobs—one at a call center, another as a server at a restaurant—but they weren't enough and they didn't fit into my primary employment schedule well.

Some good news started to take shape. We were able to re-modify our mortgage down to a lower monthly payment, and build a plan to avoid foreclosure. Then, I picked up a job cleaning daycare centers at night. I'd work my day job from 9 a.m. to 5 p.m., and then clean two daycare centers from 9 p.m. to 5 a.m. Briana would often fill in for me if I had a big meeting the next day, had to travel, or was just too tired. It was hard, but we were thankful. God was revealing a plan to get us through a difficult season, and we felt hope in our situation.

When you're awake and alone every night, you get a chance to do a lot of thinking. I was thankful to have a solution for our financial woes, but I was also very angry. I was angry at myself. I was angry at the Ponzi scheme. And, I was angry at God.

"How could you let this happen? "I cried out to Him. "Why didn't you stop me? I was just trying to help my family!"

With tears streaming down my face in the middle of the night, carrying 20 pounds of dirty diapers to the dumpster, I heard God speak.

"It's good to hear your voice, son," I heard Him say in my heart. "Son." That one word wrecked me. God was talking to me as He saw me, His child, even if I didn't see myself the same as He did yet. God was just waiting for me to receive our Father-son relationship.

"Ryan, you had good intentions, but they weren't My intentions," He continued. "I never wanted any of this for you, and My heart is breaking for you. But I've got you because I love you. You matter to me. Trust me. I will not only get you through this, but I've got great things in store for you. Let's spend time together. Do you trust Me?"

He highlighted the scriptures Proverbs 3:5-6, and those verses have become tattooed on my heart: "Trust in the Lord with all your heart and lean not on your own understanding. In all your ways acknowledge Him, and He will make your paths straight."

God was showing me the gift is not where He will take me, the gift is our "yada" relationship. It is our journey together. What happens along the way is just the manifestation of a Father and son spending time together—walking and talking together, laughing, crying, and dreaming together.

He asked me to trust Him that night at the daycare center, and I said "yes." It was a simple "yes," but my surrendered response changed everything in my life.

That night, as the dark gave way to the light of the morning, I felt my tears of intense sorrow turn to unspeakable joy. It was Psalm 30:5 in real-time: "Weeping may endure for a night, but joy comes in the morning."

Sometimes the Lord will remind me of our conversations at the daycare centers, especially if I've unintentionally prioritized other areas of my life over my relationship with Him. He doesn't do this to strike fear in my heart, but to remind me of how wonderful it is when we spend time together. The Lord desires relationship with His children.

As grateful as we were to have the daycare center cleaning gig, it wasn't sustainable for the long haul. I was in my first six months of my new job building and managing strategic partnerships in North Texas, Oklahoma and Arkansas for Kaplan, and I had a very clear-cut performance matrix. I loved it because I knew exactly how many enrollments I needed to produce in a six-month period to make a specific salary for the following six months.

I was very aware of the increase in salary I needed to cover the amount we were bringing in from cleaning the daycare centers. December of 2009 was the last month of my first six-month period. I had done really well, but I still needed ten enrollments to hit my target salary number. For context, seven enrollments was a great month for my role.

For those of you who have been in any type of business-to-business (B2B) sales role, you know that December is appropriately known as "dead month." That's code for "no sales," because most companies are navigating holiday time-off for their employees and waiting until January to pick up partner initiatives that aren't of the highest priority.

The first two weeks of December rolled by, and I didn't have a single enrollment. Not a single one.

I tried everything–calling old leads, going door-to-door in my territory, setting up tables at community events on the weekends. Still, nothing.

Heading into the last two weeks of December I had zero enrollments, and those last two weeks were the week of Christmas and the week between Christmas and New Year's Day. If December is considered the "dead month," then the last two weeks of December should be considered the deadest of all dead weeks in the deadest month of the year.

THE GOD OF TECH

I got alone with God. "What do I do?" I asked. It was more of a plea than a question.

"Verizon," He responded. At that moment, I knew exactly what I was supposed to do. And I knew it was from God. Ever since our encounter in the daycare center, He and I had been talking to each other every day. I recognized His voice, and that gave me total peace and confidence to trust and obey what He was saying to me.

Verizon was one of our corporate partners, and the company had a phenomenal employee tuition assistance program. A lot of companies will reimburse employees for college education once they complete courses, but Verizon went a step further. Its employee education benefit covered courses up front, with a cap of roughly $8,000/year for employees to get their college degrees. To this day, it's one of the best corporate employee education benefits in the country, and even the employees at the local corporate retail stores are eligible.

I knew I wasn't going to have much luck with Verizon's corporate call centers or regional corporate offices because of the holidays, but I knew the retail stores were in full swing. I worked retail in high school and college, and my busiest work schedules were always in December. I figured all of their employees were working a lot of hours, and could use a little hope for the New Year.

Taking the word God gave me, I immediately started calling every Verizon corporate retail store in my territory. I would ask the manager if he or she would be so kind to spend five minutes in their next Friday morning staff meeting to let employees know about our partnership (we offered a partner tuition reduction), how they could utilize their employee education benefit and get their degrees for free, and remind them that January was a great time to go back to school.

I had a number of managers agree, and so I sent them a simple one-pager with bullet points. The enrollments started coming in, and on December 31st at 4:30 p.m., I secured my 10th enrollment for the month. I hit my mark for the exact salary increase I needed to go down to one job. God is so good!

"This is a miracle!" people throughout our organization would say, referring to what had happened. The Verizon miracle became a significant SQ moment in my life.

My Senior Vice President (SVP) took note, and called me to see how I did it. I told him the truth. I told him that I prayed, and God gave me the word "Verizon."

I had never spent more than five minutes with the SVP before, and here I was telling him it was all because of a word from God. The funny thing was, he believed me. I remember him saying it had to be God because it just didn't make any sense to get those numbers in the last two weeks of December.

This was the start of a very significant relationship in my life. My SVP asked me to teach the rest of the field reps how to employ what quickly became known as the "Verizon strategy." I was highlighted as a high-potential leadership employee by my director and SVP, and I was asked to join leadership meetings and speak into decisions for the future of our organization.

Meanwhile, my wife and I were expecting our second child, and my enrollment numbers were soaring. The next six months, I got another significant salary increase, and we were starting to pay down a lot of the debt we had incurred with the failed investment.

God had taken us from barely surviving to thriving, but it was all the fruit of our intimate relationship with Him. My wife and I started having these amazing couch conversations where we invited the Holy Spirit into our talks, and He would give us dreams, thoughts and ideas. It was so naturally supernatural.

It was a much different story heading into December 2010 than it was heading into the previous December. I had hit my max number of enrollments for the period, and was expecting the highest possible salary for my position after the first of the year.

But then a funny thing happened on the way to another salary increase. The Department of Education (DOE) ran an undercover audit of for-profit education institutions in 2010, and some unethical admission practices from a few schools in the industry caused an overhaul of government regulation for the entire industry. The DOE restricted schools from compensating employees based on the number of enrollments they brought in.

Kaplan was a for-profit university, and our organization's entire compensation model was shut down a month before I was slated to get the highest salary for my role. My team and I were stuck in a state of paralysis, trying to figure out what was compliant with the DOE.

Early in 2011, my employer sent out a corporate-wide email talking about re-organization and severance packages for volunteer resignation. We all knew what that meant. It was time to update our resumes and start looking for other jobs.

My SVP, the one who reached out to me about the Verizon strategy, left the company, and the new head of our business unit requested a meeting with me. I thought I was toast, but much to my surprise, he offered me a promotion to become the Director of the Central Region for Field Operations. It was less in pay than I was set to make with my projected salary increase before the DOE audit; but it was still really good, and more than enough to pay the bills.

I felt relieved, but I didn't feel peace. I shared the news with Briana, leaving out the part that I didn't feel one hundred percent about taking the job. I think I was feeling a little PTSD from being in the pit of financial despair after the failed investment, and I was afraid to think about what would happen if we didn't have enough income again. I was willing to settle for safety, at that point. But, the safest place you can be is always where God leads you, even if it feels contrary to natural logic.

Briana prayed about it, and God told her I wasn't supposed to take the job. We talked about it, and quite frankly I was hesitant. But, I knew she was right. God was saying the same thing to me.

I asked God what we should do next, and He was silent. Perhaps when God is silent, the silence is actually His voice. In the silence I found a new depth of total trust in my loving Father. I didn't know what was next, but I knew God had a plan in store, and it was bigger than me taking the promotion at Kaplan.

With the real estate debacle, I blew past the warning signs because I wasn't willing to accept that God was speaking to me and telling me not to sign the deal. In essence I was saying to God, "Trust me. I got this."

Now, I was saying to God, "I trust You. You've got this. I can't see the next step, but I know You've got me in the palm of Your hand, and You're taking good care of us."

I said "no" to fear and "yes" to God. These "yeses" to God were getting clearer and clearer in my heart and mind. I recognized the voice of my Father, and I followed it. Ironically, what He was asking me to say "yes" to seemed to require even more faith than the "yes" before.

"I'm not going to take the job," I told my boss. He was stunned, and asked what I had lined up instead. "I'm not sure," I replied. "But, my wife and I prayed about it, and we feel like we're not supposed to take this position. Thank you so much for the offer."

And just like that, I took the severance package, and set out for the unknown. About two months after I resigned, I received a call from my former SVP. He was on the ground floor of an EdTech startup that had the potential to be a major disruptor in Higher Education. The company was called StraighterLine, and it offered general education college courses online for a fraction of the time and cost of colleges and universities. For example, a student could take a 100-level microeconomics course for $150, complete it in 30 days, and transfer the credits to a degree-granting university. Each course saved students up to 90 percent compared to the same course at the college in which they were transferring the credits.

My former SVP was overseeing strategic initiatives, and he asked if I'd be open to coming on board to run corporate partnerships. Sounded great, but there was a kicker: the company was in early-stage investment funding, and it didn't have the budget to pay me a salary. My compensation would be 100 percent commission directly tied to corporate partnerships I signed.

And there was a kicker on top of the kicker. Because StraighterLine was so new and different, companies had no HR guidelines to partner with us. In the world of corporate-higher education partnerships, the top two requirements are that the institution has to be accredited and offer degrees. StraighterLine didn't check either of those boxes.

So, in summation: I was asked to run corporate partnerships entirely on commission tied to partnerships signed, and companies had HR policy that restricted them from signing partnerships with a company like StraighterLine. If I was going to succeed, I was going to first have to educate the prospective clients, create demand, and cut through the red tape of HR policy. I might as well have thrown in a triathlon for good measure.

But I really loved my SVP, and I considered him to be a great leader and mentor. He was and is hands-down the best person I've ever seen develop strategic B2B partnerships. Plus, I loved the heart and vision of the CEO to help people.

When I told Briana about the opportunity, she said it didn't make any sense in the natural, but she felt the Holy Spirit was saying to take the job. I heard Him say the same thing. I knew it seemed completely crazy from the outside looking in, but we knew God was directing our path and we knew this was where He was leading us.

So, we said "yes."

I wish I could tell you it was all daisies and daffodils after I took the StraighterLine job, but the truth is I went four months without signing a single partnership. That meant I went six months without any income; and yet, God always provided.

There were times when I would just lay on my bedroom floor, with what felt like a four-ton boulder of stress on my chest, because in the natural things we're looking scary. But I kept hearing God say, "Just trust Me."

I knew if I could get one partnership, others would follow. And that's exactly what happened.

I signed one partnership, then another, and another. At the end of the year, I had 20 partnerships. When I looked back at what I made in that year, it was $60 thousand more than I would have made had I stayed at Kaplan. Also, a year after I left, Kaplan completely dissolved the department I was offered a promotion in.

God was again blessing us in the season, but then He started to reveal a deeper revelation to me. He had been providing for us in these seasons, and simultaneously preparing us for what He had in store for us down the road.

It wasn't just that we were being financially blessed. In the matter of one career move, I went from working with local and regional managers on partnerships to sitting down with high-level executives at some of the largest companies in the world to collaborate on their employee talent and development initiatives. Even more, I was learning from an expert about what it looks like to build a strategic partnership.

After two and a half years at StraighterLine, I transitioned to another higher education company called The Learning House (TLH) that built and managed online degree programs for colleges and universities across the country. My role was to sign and oversee corporate education partnerships with large companies that leveraged our online degree programs to help upskill and reskill employees for career advancement.

Around that time, we moved from Dallas, TX to Oklahoma City, OK to help plant a church as volunteers. I was working my corporate job 50-plus hours a week and spending another 10-15 hours helping to build the church. Timewise it was a lot, but it didn't feel that way. Whatever God calls you to do, He will give you the grace to do it.

About a year into my role, The Learning House acquired a coding bootcamp out of Akron, OH called The Software Guild that taught people how to code in as little as twelve weeks, so they could land jobs as software developers. To be honest, I don't think I'd ever heard of a coding bootcamp before then; but as part of my job, I was responsible for leveraging The Guild with existing and future corporate partners.

Overnight, it felt like my partnerships with companies like IBM, Liberty Mutual and AT&T shifted from utilizing our degree programs with colleges and universities to wanting to hire graduates from our coding bootcamp and using our software development program to reskill and upskill their current employees for the future of work.

There was (and still is) a massive demand for tech talent in the workspace. At the time, in 2015, there was only one qualified candidate for every three open tech jobs, and IBM projected a 1 million-job shortfall in tech over the next five years. Regardless of industry, every company was falling over themselves to find qualified tech talent, and the current pool of Computer Science (CS) degree graduates from colleges and universities wasn't making a dent in the talent gap. Furthermore, CS grads from universities not named Stanford and MIT, often didn't possess the immediately applicable skills needed to become a junior software developer.

In 2016, I helped lead a TechHire grant in Queens, NY that provided in-demand tech skills to an underserved and underrepresented community so individuals could land high-paying, high-growth careers in tech. As part of the initiative, we built a 16-week program that focused on teaching a coding language called Java.

The program was an incredible source of hope for the community. For example, we would have single mothers bus into our campus where we also provided daycare for their children while they were in class. Three months after completing the program, we'd have graduates, including some of those single moms, go from making minimum wage to over $80k as a software developer. The results were life-changing!

I remember thinking to myself, "This is how you transform communities." And as soon as I thought that, I heard the Lord say, "You're right. Would you build something like this with Me, so that people didn't just discover what they're capable of, but they discovered their identity as my children?"

God gripped me with the revelation that, as the Church, our minimum expectation was to give someone in need a fish to eat. In Matthew 25:31-46, we see Jesus give us a mandate to feed, shelter and clothe the poor. In fact, He says those who do this are His righteous people who will have everlasting life. Those who don't help the poor represent the nature of the enemy and are destined for the same fate as the devil in eternal punishment.

Not coincidentally, it was after this message that the

religious leaders went to Caiaphas, the high priest, and plotted to kill Jesus. Instead of rising to the call of righteousness, they callused their hearts in religious pride.

We cannot ever veer from our call to be the hands and feet of Jesus, taking care of those in need. But, from that foundational truth, what if we could take it another level and teach a person in need how to fish, equipping and empowering them to create healthy, thriving ecosystems for themselves and future generations?

That was the question I was asking myself, and that's all the Lord needed to create with me to manifest His will on earth as it is in heaven. It's what Bishop T.D. Jakes calls, "Putting the things in the room to make hope happen."

In the TechHire grant narrative, the underserved communities were identified as "at-risk." That never sat well with me.

My wife, Briana, says something that has greatly impacted my perspective on life, "It's the subtle undertones that create culture." The words we use matter, and if we are going to identify an underserved community as a risk, then that is exactly how we will approach it– from a distance, as a charity case void of authentic relationship.

I believe humans have an inherent longing to be seen as their Creator sees them. God says, "I know the plans I have for you; plans to prosper you and not to harm you, plans to give you hope and a future." (Jeremiah 29:11).

These communities are not a risk, but a people of hope with a promise of peace, protection and prosperity from the Lord. These aren't at-risk communities; they are at-hope communities!

God asked me to build something with Him that

THE GOD OF TECH

magnifies His love, so that all would taste and see His goodness. I replied with a simple "yes"; and in that moment, God planted the seed of Bethel School of Technology in my heart. I just didn't know it yet.

My mission was and always will be to bring the love of Christ to everyone, everywhere. I know, as I hope you do, that one encounter with His love will completely change a person's life. Jesus fulfilled the prophecy of Isaiah of the one who would bring good news to the poor, heal the brokenhearted, proclaim liberty to the captives, give new eyes for the blind to see, and set the oppressed free (Luke 4:18).

That same Jesus lives in you and me, and we get to carry that power and authority wherever we go. From the fruit I saw in the Queens, NY TechHire project, and knowing the goodness of God in my own life, I had the radical belief that we could transform a community through Christ-centered in-demand skills training. And if we could transform enough communities, then we could transform entire cities, states, and nations!

The Lord put the seed in my heart to build a Christ-centered coding school, but He didn't give me a full picture of the path. I'm convinced that when you pioneer with God to build something new, the path appears with each step you take with Him. But once the path is created, it serves as a roadmap for others to follow.

It's like Google Maps recognizing a new home. Before the home is built, it can be difficult to get proper directions from Google to the property. But once the home is built and becomes someone's residence, Google registers it in its database and provides clear directions to the location.

As Holy Spirit-led innovators, we get to build a home for

the kingdom of heaven on earth and show others how to get there. It's like Frideswide's well appearing when she prayed for God to move; it became a healing well for generations to come. It's like Maxwell discovering that information can be transferred from one place to the next through electromagnetic waves; it now serves as the foundation for our modern technology.

The best way I can illustrate my "yada" relationship with the Lord is from a scene in *Indiana Jones and the Last Crusade*. In his search for the holy grail, Indiana Jones comes to a deep canyon he is supposed to cross, but there is no way to get to the other side. A legend of the map to the holy grail shows a bridge across the canyon, and Jones realizes the bridge must be invisible. With radical faith, he takes a step. As his feet make contact with the unseen bridge, a plank appears. Another plank appears with each step, allowing him to reach the other side.

A few months after the Lord spoke to me about building a tech training program with Him, He uncovered the next step. I was on a business trip, driving back home to Oklahoma City from Dallas. It was late afternoon, and as I looked at the sky, it reminded me of a California-blue sky. As soon as I thought that, I heard the Lord say, "I'm giving you California."

I went home, and said nothing to my wife about the word God gave me. About a week later, she asked me if God was saying something to me about California. I told her what he shared with me on my trip home from Dallas, and she said He said the same thing to her, with the exact phrasing, "I'm giving you California."

Not long after that, God gave us more direction about California, specifically highlighting Redding in our hearts. The only thing I knew about Redding was that Bethel Church was located there. And I didn't know that much about Bethel Church.

I knew of Bethel Music. Our church (and nearly every church in Oklahoma City, for that matter) sang Bethel Music songs on Sunday during worship.

My wife had introduced me to Bethel through Danny Silk's book, *Loving Our Kids on Purpose*. It confirmed what God had been speaking to Briana on how we should be raising our children: through honor and empowering love, instead of the "punishment and control" paradigm that was so prevalent in our environment.

There was a story Danny shared in his book about his friend, Kris Vallotton. Danny's teenage daughter had gone missing, and Danny called Kris to pray. When he prayed, God gave Kris a word of knowledge, in which he saw a vision of Danny's daughter at a local park. Sure enough, Danny's daughter was at the park where she was meeting up with a boy that she had met online.

I knew little about the prophetic, and nothing about words of knowledge at that time, but I was drawn to how God used Kris to rescue Danny's daughter. I started reading Kris's latest book at the time, *Destined to Win*. In it he spoke of his mentor and friend, Bill Johnson, who displayed an unwavering desire to continually seek the presence of the Lord and please the Father. It is from that communion relationship that Bethel has changed the world—healing the sick, delivering the oppressed, bringing good news to the poor, and preaching the kingdom of heaven to all the ends of the earth.

Briana and I prayed together, and the Holy Spirit

confirmed Redding to both of us. God had also given her a word shortly after we moved to Oklahoma City that we would be there for two and a half years. When we moved to Redding, it was exactly two and a half years.

Once we said "yes" to Redding, God revealed the next plank of the invisible bridge. I assumed I would continue to work at The Learning House. In fact, I had already asked my boss if I could work on the West Coast, and he had given his approval.

But one Sunday morning at church, I was sharing a pre-service message to our volunteer team. When I got off the stage, Briana said the Lord told her I was going to be on staff at Bethel Church.

We knew nobody at Bethel, and I wasn't the type of person to force my way into an environment, certainly not a church. Right after Briana shared that word with me, the Lord reminded me of our conversation about transforming communities through Christ-centered tech education.

I knew it was time to step out into the unknown and start something new. I was connected to a man named Michael Clifford on LinkedIn, who is a major influencer in the online higher education space. He and his business partner had bought a small, nearly bankrupt Christian university in Phoenix, Arizona called Grand Canyon University years ago, and turned it into one of the largest and most successful online universities in the world.

I had actually written a paper on Michael about the online disruption of higher education for a graduate class, but we didn't know each other. He was just one of those thousands of connections you accept on social media, without really knowing the person.

Michael was sharing a number of articles about coding bootcamps on LinkedIn, which caught my eye, since I was involved in the same space. Then, he posted a picture of himself with Bill Johnson, and I felt compelled to reach out to him in a direct message.

In a couple of paragraphs, I shared my story and how God was calling us to Redding. I felt something on this connection. In my heart, it felt the same as the Lord asking me to trust Him in the daycare centers, giving me the Verizon word, and calling me to walk away from Kaplan and take the StraighterLine job.

It was a Friday afternoon when I messaged Michael, and later that evening he responded. We jumped on a call the next day.

I was a little nervous, to say the least. I knew this guy was a heavy hitter in the education space. But Michael is different. He sees what other people don't, and makes time for everyone who is driven to represent Jesus in the marketplace.

When I shared in detail what God had done in our lives and how He was calling us to Redding, Michael said this was a Kairos moment. He said that he had been speaking to Kris Vallotton from Bethel about building the first-ever Christian coding bootcamp, and they had been praying for someone to come into the environment who could run it.

After 15 minutes of conversation with Michael, he said I was the guy to run the school. "What exactly do you mean?" I asked. "I want you to be the CEO of Bethel Tech," he replied.

Just like that, another plank in the invisible bridge appeared, and it was all making sense as to why God was calling us to Redding. It was a Kairos moment, indeed.

After talking to Briana and praying together, we felt the Lord was on this, and we said "yes." I hope, by now, you're seeing a theme. Saying "yes" to the Lord creates a pathway for God to manifest His will on earth as it is in heaven.

We moved to Redding in September 2017, and launched our first class at Bethel Tech in January 2018. In addition to in-demand tech skills, we embedded a spiritual component that taught students how to build healthy relationships and community, create a culture of honor, engage in brave communication and conflict resolution, and display nobility and accountability in the workplace. These are Kingdom values, but they're also the same character skills in which companies are investing millions of dollars to improve workplace culture.

Quickly, we had an open door to some of the leading tech companies in the world, like Facebook, Google, LinkedIn, Microsoft, and Salesforce—specifically because of our intentional focus on high-character. In over four years, we have seen students go from no tech experience and making minimum wage to landing jobs making over $100 thousand less than three months after graduation.

We've seen a woman reconcile with her estranged mother, with whom she hadn't spoken in twenty years, after an honor and forgiveness activation in our revival group. Forgiveness is often a key to physical healing, and shortly after our student reconciled with her mother, she was scheduled to have surgery on a detached retina. When she went in for her pre-operation, her retina had miraculously re-attached on its own, and she didn't need surgery. The doctor couldn't believe it!

We've seen a student discover and walk in his identity as an heir to God and ambassador of Christ and pray a woman back to life. The student was vacationing at a beach when he noticed a woman fall off her surfboard and go underwater. Without hesitation, he jumped into the water and swam to rescue the woman. By the time he got to her, she had stopped breathing. He brought her back to the shore, and called the emergency paramedics.

As he and others waited for the ambulance to arrive, the woman turned blue. She was not breathing for over 30 minutes and she had no pulse, but our student prayed over the woman and declared in the name of Jesus for her to come back to life. Immediately, she started breathing again! He said he never would have had the faith to do what Jesus did had he not discovered His identity in Christ through our program.

Jesus sent His disciples out to declare the kingdom of heaven at hand and display its superior reality on earth—to heal the sick, cleanse the lepers, raise the dead, and cast out demons (Matthew 10:7-8). Our Bethel Tech student did the same, and a life was saved.

We've been a part of our student, Eno Chen's, Holy Spirit-led moonshot journey to usher the presence of God into the healthcare industry. In her Bethel Tech admissions application, Eno wrote that she dreamed about using data science to eradicate pediatric diseases. Prior to starting our program, Eno was a full-time mom with no background in technology. She also had an overwhelming fear of public settings and social interactions. So much so, that she was too afraid to get her driver's license because she didn't want to drive in public.

But she had a dream to change the world through the love of Christ, and she said "yes" to God's call on her life. Eno excelled in our data science program. She was naturally and supernaturally gifted for tech, but it was her spiritual breakthrough that was so incredible.

In her revival group, she received a profound revelation of her identity in Christ. She discovered that God's grace empowered her to see herself as God does– fearfully and wonderfully made, designed on purpose and for a purpose.

Walking in her God-given identity, Eno's belief system was transformed. She got her driver's license, conquered her life-long fear of driving, and began to confidently reach out to potential employers for job opportunities.

Two weeks after graduation, she landed a job as a Data Analyst at Seattle Children's Hospital. In an email, the CEO welcomed her to a team that was committed to eradicating pediatric disease. It was the exact wording she shared in her Bethel Tech application!

Since then, she has been promoted, and recently she received a moonshot idea from God to create a data dashboard that is revolutionizing the way the healthcare industry organizes and tracks organ donor and recipient matches. She also just started a prayer group with other Christians at her company. Eno operated with the mind of Christ; and through spiritual intelligence, she partnered with the Holy Spirit to conceive a third-heaven solution for a first-heaven problem.

Also, I'm excited to say that Bethel Tech recently started an At-Hope initiative providing scholarships for underserved, underrepresented individuals. We've seen sex-traffic survivors learn to code and get great jobs and promotions in the tech field. We've had a homeless student, who was once addicted to drugs, excel in our program and start a successful web design business. We've had single moms go from working multiple jobs, living paycheck to paycheck and barely making ends meet, to making over $80 thousand a year as junior developers - just like the TechHire initiative in Queens, NY!

And we're just getting started. We're working with a large non-profit group that provides food, clothing and shelter to individuals in developing communities across the globe to help women in the Philippines and India learn to code and get tech jobs. We're partnering with a church in Chicago that is excellent at finding jobs for residents in one of the most underserved areas of the city. We're talking to cities and developing countries about transforming their communities through character-focused tech education.

I'm convinced this is just a taste of the great things we're going to do with the Lord to show His goodness to all of His children. The Lord will take your surrendered "yes" and multiply it further than your imagination and ability could ever take you. It is His Spirit-led moonshot ideas that move humanity heavenward.

These testimonies never get old, and just writing them down brings me so much life and joy knowing how good the Father is to and through His children. The Hebrew word "edut" (pronounced "ay-dooth") for testimony means to do it again. And the testimony of Jesus is the spirit of prophecy. His Spirit resides in us, and He said:

> Whoever believes in me, the works I do he will do also; and greater works than these he will do, because I go to My Father. Whatever you ask in My name, that I will do, that the Father may be glorified in the Son. If you ask anything in My name, I will do it. (John 14:12-14 NKJV)

We can be confident that the things Jesus did on earth, we too will do and see because the Lord is faithful to His Word. Everything flows from an intimate relationship with the Father. It is through the relationship that we have the mind of Christ, operate with spiritual intelligence, receive downloads from the Lord that serve as the foundation of moonshot ideas, and ultimately partner with Him to bring His superior reality on earth as it is in heaven.

I think back to my personal journey with the Lord, and I'm overwhelmed with how much the Lord can do with a "yes." From my encounters with the Lord at the daycare centers to starting Bethel Tech and our incredible student testimonies—God is a mastermind at fitting our stories together to unveil His desire for all of humanity to rediscover the origin of their existence as His sons and daughters.

A history with the Lord is not a compilation of mutually exclusive events, like a curated Spotify playlist of our favorite God moments. Rather, each moment of God's goodness in our lives is interlinked to fulfill the story He has written on our lives from the beginning of time. They are reminders that His goodness is never-ending, and His desire is a deep relationship with His children.

10

ONE RED DOT

"For the earth will be filled with the knowledge of the glory of the Lord, as the waters cover the sea." Habakkuk 2:14 NKJV

In 2015, two years before starting Bethel Tech, I was at Cisco's headquarters in Silicon Valley as part of a group discussing workplace trends and culture. Cisco delivers high-technology services and products in areas like the Internet of Things (IoT), domain security, and videoconferencing. With 80,000 employees, it is one of the largest IT companies in the world.

During one of our sessions, Cisco's VP of Human Resources shared a satellite view of the globe. On it were thousands of tiny dots of light. Most of the dots were tiny yellow lights, but some of the dots were red and much larger than the yellow dots.

As the presenter zoomed in, I could see the big red dots were connected to multiple dots across the globe. The presenter explained that each dot represented one of Cisco's 80 thousand employees, and he referred to the big red dots as nodes because of their high-connectivity to multiple areas of the organization.

The presenter then shared how Cisco was about to launch a highly-focused initiative to instill the company's core values into its entire workforce. They knew it would be impossible for the HR team to spend time with all 80 thousand employees individually.

But those big red nodes.

Cisco's HR team was convinced it could spread the company's core values to every employee and improve workplace culture if it was intentional about spending focused time with the most connected individuals within their organization. The leadership team set out to make the big red nodes their culture apostles.

As the presenter shared more about the initiative, I had a vision from God. He showed me a view of earth just like the one Cisco's VP of HR shared at the beginning of his presentation.

Just like the Cisco map, there was a sea of dots lighting up the globe. And just like the Cisco map, there were red dots noticeably bigger than the smaller yellow dots.

The Lord then zoomed in on the map, and the red dots were highly connected to dots across the world. He showed me that the dots represented the Body of Christ, and the red nodes, were believers, who had postured their hearts in total surrender to His will to bring heaven to earth. They were the ones who were listening, trusting and obeying His voice to share His love to all the ends of the earth by partnering with other believers so that everyone would taste and see His goodness.

Then He showed me the yellow light dots getting bigger and turning into red nodes. First, there were a few. Then, more and more until all you could see was red nodes, and they bled together to form one big red dot that covered the globe. The big red dot was the redeeming blood of Jesus that restored humankind to its original design as sons and daughters of the Creator of the universe—their heavenly Father, who loved them deeply.

The Lord told me that the time had come for the Church, the Body of Christ, to be fully actualized. A new season was approaching where individual parts of His Body would no longer work separately, but would grow in wisdom, love and authority as they connected with one another and operated in their God-given gifts for the good of all humanity.

He showed me that the red nodes would catalyze the yellow dots to believe all things are possible with God, and more yellow dots would continue to pop up and turn into red nodes as the gospel was shared across the world. He told me the initial red nodes were trailblazers taking new territory by engaging all spheres of society, specifically highlighting the tech space as a major player in activating this next great movement of God.

Halfway through writing this book, as I was recalling the Cisco vision in my mind, the Lord reminded me of the story of Nehemiah rebuilding the walls of Jerusalem. In 589 BC, the Israelites were taken into captivity by the Babylonian empire, and the city of Jerusalem was destroyed. Fifty years later, the Babylonians fell to the Persians, whose Emperor, Cyrus the Great, decreed the rebuilding of the city of Jerusalem in 539 BC. For 92 years, the Jews tried to rebuild the city, starting with the walls of protection, but foreign opposition and lack of vision stalled the process.

Nehemiah was the cupbearer to Artaxerxes, King of Persia, and he was given written authority by the king to rebuild the city of Jerusalem around 444 BC. As one of the king's most trusted court members, Nehemiah, a Jew, had great favor and protection to do the job. He brought hope to the Jews still living in or near Jerusalem, and strategically banded them together as family to rebuild the walls at an accelerated rate. In 52 days, Nehemiah, who was not a builder by trade, led the complete rebuild of the walls. What had taken the Jews nearly a century to no avail, took Nehemiah less than two months to coordinate.

How did that happen? Like Frideswide, Maxwell, and so many of the other individuals I've mentioned in this book, Nehemiah partnered with God to manifest third heaven solutions for first heaven problems. His seemingly impossible feat was the fruit of his "yada" relationship and spiritual intelligence with the Lord.

The completion of the walls of Jerusalem reignited a sense of unity among the Israelites, who had forgotten their identity as people of God and were a scattered remnant of a once-mighty nation. By the droves, the Israelites returned to Jerusalem from other lands to be together again. Around 50 thousand Israelites returned to Jerusalem, and together they began to rebuild the city inside the walls (Nehemiah 7:66-67).

Once all together, Nehemiah had the scribe Ezra read the law of Moses first given to the Israelites by God a thousand years prior. The Word of the Lord pierced the hearts of the Israelites who were generations removed from even knowing their heritage as God's people. They fell on their faces worshiping God, weeping that they had replaced Him with false gods. They repented for trading in the one true God, who is the Author of life, for a counterfeit solution from the enemy, who sought to destroy them.

Then Ezra and Nehemiah, in obedience to God, had compassion on the Israelites. Instead of condemning them for their sin, Ezra and Nehemiah reminded them of their right-standing as people of God and celebrated their repentance. Here is what they shared:

> This day is holy to the Lord your God; do not mourn nor weep. Go your way, eat the fat, drink the sweet, and send portions to those for whom nothing is prepared; for this day is holy to our Lord. Do not sorrow, for the joy of the Lord is your strength. (Nehemiah 8:9-10 NKJV)

The day was holy because the people of God had rediscovered their origin of existence. The Jews were encountering the love of a good Father, who designed each one of them on purpose and for a purpose since the beginning of creation. They were the source of His joy, and His joy was the source of their strength. This is the state of human be-ing that can only come from one's intimate relationship with the Creator. Creation and Creator are inextricably and eternally entangled in joyful relationship with each other.

The rebuild of the wall was not so the Israelites could celebrate their own ingenuity. It wasn't a moonshot for the sake of doing something difficult no one had ever achieved before.

It was done to bring the people of God back together as one so they could encounter the love of God and rediscover their royal identities in Him. It was done in such an impossible way that everyone had to acknowledge it could only have been accomplished in partnership with God. It was done to move humanity heavenward.

Then the Lord brought me back to the Cisco vision. He told me there would be an acceleration to this unifying movement of God, much like Nehemiah rebuilding the wall of Jerusalem, as more and more yellow dots worked together with each other and with the red nodes. The yellow dots would turn into red nodes, and the flywheel of revival would gain momentum as the Body of Christ re-dug the wells of Living Water and tore down the walls that had divided the Church. Once unified, this fully actualized Body, with Christ as its head, would be unstoppable. The gates of hell would not be able to stand against it.

Then the Lord told me the flywheel of revival would shift to a global reformation through the use of technology as the veil that had for so long blinded people from realizing their true identities as His children was lifted. The earth would be filled with the knowledge of the glory of the Lord, as millions of people, and even entire nations, would rediscover their origin of existence and taste and see that the Lord is good.

Through this enlightenment of God's goodness, they would repent and enter into an eternal "yada" relationship with their loving Father—not out of compliance or obligation, but from an overwhelming sense of joy. They would know that they were God's children and that He created all things in Jesus, on purpose and for relationship with Him.

"For in Him all things were created: things in heaven and on earth, visible and invisible, whether thrones or powers or rulers or authorities; all things have been created through Him and for Him. He is before all things, and in Him all things hold together." (Colossians 1:16-17 NIV)

Or, in the words of Frideswide: whatever is not God is nothing.

Including technology.

Because He is the God of tech.

ABOUT THE AUTHOR

Ryan Collins is the CEO of Bethel School of Technology and President of Bethel College in Redding, CA. He earned his Bachelor's in Journalism degree from the University of Missouri-Columbia, and has written for a number of national publications, including *American Way*, *Charisma*, and *D Magazine*. He also wrote an excerpt for Kris Vallotton's best-selling book, *Spiritual Intelligence*.

Prior to starting Bethel Tech, Collins spent over a decade building corporate education partnerships with Fortune-level companies. He and his wife, Briana, have been married since 2005, and have three daughters.

To learn more or to book Ryan, visit: www.ryancollins.info.

WORKS CITED

1. Ford, David Nash. "St. Frideswide, Patroness of Oxfordshire or Berkshire?," Nash Ford Publishing, accessed October 1, 2020, www.berkshirehistory.com/legends/frideswide01.html.

2. Babbage, Charles, and Martin Campbell-Kelly. *Charles Babbage: Passages from the Life of a Philosopher*. Rutgers University Press, 1994, p. 402.

3. Babbage, Charles, and Martin Campbell-Kelly. *Charles Babbage: Passages from the Life of a Philosopher*. Rutgers University Press, 1994, p. 396.

4. Sharlin, Harold I.. "William Thomson, Baron Kelvin". Encyclopedia Britannica, 13 Dec. 2022, www.britannica.com/biography/William-Thomson-Baron-Kelvin. Accessed 12 February 2023.

5. Sharlin, Harold I.. "William Thomson, Baron Kelvin". Encyclopedia Britannica, 13 Dec. 2022, https://www.britannica.com/biography/William-Thomson-Baron-Kelvin. Accessed 12 February 2023.

6. Lord Kelvin, quoted in *Twelfth Report of the Committee of the Christian Evidence Society* (London: G. Norman and Son, 1883), p. 46.

7. Britannica, The Editors of Encyclopaedia. "Faraday's law of induction". Encyclopedia Britannica, 17 Nov. 2022, https://www.britannica.com/science/Faradays-law-of-induction. Accessed 12 February 2023.

8. Cantor, G.N.. (1985). Reading the Book of Nature: The Relation Between Faraday's Religion and his Science. In: Gooding, D., James, F.A.J.L. (eds) Faraday Rediscovered. Palgrave, London. https://doi.org/10.1007/978-1-349-11139-8_5, p. 71.

9. Glazebrook, Richard. *James Clerk Maxwell and Modern Physics*. Project Gutenberg, p. 9.

10. Campbell, Lewis. *The Life of James Clerk Maxwell*. London: MacMillan and Co, 1882, p. 96

11. "James Clerk Maxwell." Famous Scientists. famousscientists.org. 01 Jul. 2014. Web. 2/12/2023 <www.famousscientists.org/james-clerk-maxwell/>.

12. "James Clerk Maxwell." Famous Scientists. famousscientists.org. 01 Jul. 2014. Web. 2/12/2023 <www.famousscientists.org/james-clerk-maxwell/>.

13. "How Heinrich Hertz Discovered Radio Waves," accessed June 11, 2021, <www.famousscientists.org/how-hertz-discovered-radio-waves/>

14. Whitney, Heather. "James Clerk Maxwell: A Model for Twenty-first Century Physics in the Christian Liberal Arts," *Christian Scholars Review*, July 15, 2016, https://christianscholars.com/james-clerk-maxwell-a-model-for-twenty-first-century-physics-in-the-christian-liberal-arts/

15. volume II; lecture 1, "Electromagnetism"; section 1-6, "Electromagnetism in science and technology"; p. 1-11 The Feynman Lectures on Physics (1964)

16. William J. Cromie, "How Darwin's finches got their beaks," July 24, 2006, *The Harvard Gazette*, https://news.harvard.edu/gazette/story/2006/07/how-darwins-finches-got-their-beaks/.

17. Darwin, Charles, 1809-1882. *On the Origin of Species by Means of Natural Selection, or Preservation of Favoured Races in the Struggle for Life*. London :John Murray, 1859, p. 332.

18. Freeman, Richard Broke, and Charles Robert Darwin. *The Works of Charles Darwin: An Annotated Bibliographical Handlist*. Dawson, 1977.

19. Darwin, Charles. *Descent of Man and Selection in Relation to Sex.* 1st ed., vol. 1, D. Appleton and Co., 1989, P.65.

20. ACLU. "State of Tennessee v. Scopes." *American Civil Liberties Union*, 9 Dec. 2010, www.aclu.org/other/state-tennessee-v-scopes.

21. Digital History. "The Scopes Trial Excerpts from the Textbook John Scopes Used in Class." *Digital History*, www.digitalhistory.uh.edu/disp_textbook.cfm?smtID=3&psid=1134.

22. Digital History. "The Scopes Trial Excerpts from the Textbook John Scopes Used in Class." *Digital History*, www.digitalhistory.uh.edu/disp_textbook.cfm?smtID=3&psid=1134.

23. Digital History. "The Scopes Trial Excerpts from the Textbook John Scopes Used in Class." *Digital History*, www.digitalhistory.uh.edu/disp_textbook.cfm?smtID=3&psid=1134.

24. Digital History. "The Scopes Trial Excerpts from the Textbook John Scopes Used in Class." *Digital History*, www.digitalhistory.uh.edu/disp_textbook.cfm?smtID=3&psid=1134.

25. Digital History. "The Scopes Trial Excerpts from the Textbook John Scopes Used in Class." *Digital History*, www.digitalhistory.uh.edu/disp_textbook.cfm?smtID=3&psid=1134.

26. Digital History. "The Scopes Trial Excerpts from the Textbook John Scopes Used in Class." *Digital History*, www.digitalhistory.uh.edu/disp_textbook.cfm?smtID=3&psid=1134.

27. Wilder-Smith, B., *The Day Nazi Germany Died*, Master Books, San Diego, CA, 1982, p. 27.

28. Bergman, Dr. Jerry. "The Darwinian Foundation of Communism." *Answers in Genesis*, Answers In Genesis, 22 Mar. 2017, answersingenesis.org/charles-darwin/racism/the-darwinian-foundation-of-communism/#fn_47.

29. Bergman, Dr. Jerry. "The Darwinian Foundation of

Communism." *Answers in Genesis*, Answers In Genesis, 22 Mar. 2017, answersingenesis.org/charles-darwin/racism/the-darwinian-foundation-of-communism/#fn_45.

30. Bergman, Dr. Jerry. "The Darwinian Foundation of Communism." *Answers in Genesis*, Answers In Genesis, 22 Mar. 2017, answersingenesis.org/charles-darwin/racism/the-darwinian-foundation-of-communism/#fn_47.

31. Britannica, The Editors of Encyclopaedia. "Margaret Sanger". *Encyclopedia Britannica*, 20 Jan. 2023, https://www.britannica.com/biography/Margaret-Sanger. Accessed 11 February 2023.

32. Students for life of America. "Planned Parenthood Facts. Copyright 2023. https://studentsforlife.org/learn/planned-parenthood-facts/

33. Douglas, E.T., *Margaret Sanger: Pioneer of the Future*, Garrett Park Press, Garret Park, MD, Pg. 130, 1975.

34. Sanger, M.H., *What Every Girl Should Know*, Belvedere Publishers, New York, p. 40, 1980. A reprint of the original 1920 edition

35. Grant, G., *Grand Illusions: The Legacy of Planned Parenthood*, Wolgemuth and Hyatt, Brentwood, TN, p. 92, 1988.

36. Washington, H.A., *Medical Apartheid: The Dark History of Medical Experimentation on Black Americans from Colonial Times to the Present*, Doubleday, New York, p. 196, 2006.

37. Bergman, Jerry. "Birth control leader Margaret Sanger: Darwinist, racist, and eugenicist." Creation.com. 3 Feb. 2017. https://creation.com/margaret-sanger-darwinian-eugenicist

38. Sanger, M.H., *Margaret Sanger: An Autobiography*, Norton, New York, pgs. 366–367, 1938.

39. Washington, H.A., Medical Apartheid: The Dark History of

Medical Experimentation on Black Americans from Colonial Times to the Present, Doubleday, New York, pg. 196, 2006.

40. Supreme Court of the United States. COMCAST CORPORATION, v. NATIONAL ASSOCIATION OF AFRICAN AMERICAN-OWNED MEDIA, ET AL., R. 19 Nov. 2018.

41. Students For Life of America. "Why We Don't Need Planned Parenthood." *Students For Life of America*, 10 Mar. 2022, studentsforlife.org/why-we-dont-need-planned-parenthood/.

42. Planned Parenthood. "Annual Report." Copyright 2023. https://www.plannedparenthood.org/about-us/facts-figures/annual-report

43. Riley, Jason L. "Let's Talk about the Black Abortion Rate." *The Wall Street Journal*, Dow Jones & Company, 10 July 2018, www.wsj.com/articles/lets-talk-about-the-black-abortion-rate-1531263697.

44. Riley, Jason L. "Let's Talk about the Black Abortion Rate." *The Wall Street Journal*, Dow Jones & Company, 10 July 2018, www.wsj.com/articles/lets-talk-about-the-black-abortion-rate-1531263697.

45. Supreme Court of the United States. COMCAST CORPORATION, v. NATIONAL ASSOCIATION OF AFRICAN AMERICAN-OWNED MEDIA, ET AL., R. 19 Nov. 2018.

46. Supreme Court of the United States. COMCAST CORPORATION, v. NATIONAL ASSOCIATION OF AFRICAN AMERICAN-OWNED MEDIA, ET AL., R. 19 Nov. 2018.

47. Parenthood, Planned. "The History & Impact of Planned Parenthood." Planned Parenthood, www.plannedparenthood.org/about-us/who-we-are/our-history.

48. (R-N.J.), Rep. Chris Smith. "Abortion Debate Entering New Arenas." *The Hill*, The Hill, 3 Feb. 2016, thehill.com/blogs/congress-

blog/politics/108219-abortion-debate-entering-new-arenas/.

49. (R-N.J.), Rep. Chris Smith. "Abortion Debate Entering New Arenas." *The Hill*, The Hill, 3 Feb. 2016, thehill.com/blogs/congress-blog/politics/108219-abortion-debate-entering-new-arenas/.

50. Kliff, Sarah, and Aatish Bhatia. "When They Warn of Rare Disorders, These Prenatal Tests Are Usually Wrong." *The New York Times*, The New York Times, 1 Jan. 2022, www.nytimes.com/2022/01/01/upshot/pregnancy-birth-genetic testing.html. https://www.nytimes.com/2022/01/04/podcasts/the-daily/prenatal-tests-pregnancy-birth.html

51. Smith, Adam. "Stephen Hawking Feared Genetic Engineering Would Create 'Superhumans.'" Metro.co.uk. Oct. 2018, metro.co.uk/2018/10/14/stephen-hawking-feared-genetic-engineering-would-create-superhumans-8036193/

52. Mandela, N. Long Walk to Freedom (1994)

53. Gibson, Kate. "These Companies Are Paying for Abortion Travel." *CBS News*, CBS Interactive, 2 July 2022, www.cbsnews.com/news/abortion-travel-companies-paying-benefits-amazon-starbucks-target/.

54. Searles, Sam. "California Governor Launches out-of-State Abortion Billboards in Austin." *Kvue.com*, ABC, 11 Oct. 2022, www.kvue.com/article/news/politics/california-governor-launches-out-of-state-abortion-billboards-in-austin/269-c6aab994-2f7b-4365-9de9-e1bb1ce9d728.

55. Ostberg, René. "transhumanism". Encyclopedia Britannica, 3 Nov. 2022, https://www.britannica.com/topic/transhumanism. Accessed 10 February 2023.

56. Ostberg, René. "transhumanism". Encyclopedia Britannica, 3 Nov. 2022, https://www.britannica.com/topic/transhumanism. Accessed 10 February 2023.

57. Harari, Yuval Noah. "Will the Future be Human?" WEF Annual Meeting, 2018. YouTube. www.youtube.com/watch?v=npfShBTNp3Q

58. Harari, Yuval Noah. "Will the Future be Human?" WEF Annual Meeting, 2018. YouTube. www.youtube.com/watch?v=npfShBTNp3Q

59. IBM.com. "What is Artificial Intelligence?" www.ibm.com/topics/artificial-intelligence

60. IBM.com. "What is Artificial Intelligence?" www.ibm.com/topics/artificial-intelligence

61. Kahn, Jeremy. "The inside story of ChatGPT: How OpenAI founder Sam Altman built the world's hottest technology with billions from Microsoft." *Fortune Magazine*. January 25, 2023. https://archive.ph/rRvx1#selection-307.0-307.124

62. Thomson, Judith. "Killing, Letting Die, and The Trolley Problem." Monist: The International Quarterly Journal of General Philosophical Inquiry, 1976. Vol. 59. Pg. 204-217.

63. Falk, Dan. "Is your brain a computer?" MIT Technology Review. 25 Aug 2021. https://www.technologyreview.com/2021/08/25/1030861/is-human-brain-computer/

64. Staughton, John. "The Human Brain Vs. Supercomputers… Which One Wins?" ScienceABC.com, 17 Jan 2022. https://www.scienceabc.com/humans/the-human-brain-vs-supercomputers-which-one-wins.html

65. Hadhazy, Adam. "How it's possible for an ordinary person to lift a car." *BBC.com,* May 2016. https://www.bbc.com/future/article/20160501-how-its-possible-for-an-ordinary-person-to-lift-a-car

66. Hadhazy, Adam. "How it's possible for an ordinary person to lift a

car." *BBC.com,* May 2016.
https://www.bbc.com/future/article/20160501-how-its-possible-for-an-ordinary-person-to-lift-a-car

67. Hadhazy, Adam. "How it's possible for an ordinary person to lift a car." *BBC.com,* May 2016.
https://www.bbc.com/future/article/20160501-how-its-possible-for-an-ordinary-person-to-lift-a-car

68. Kahn, Jeremy. "The inside story of ChatGPT: How OpenAI founder Sam Altman built the world's hottest technology with billions from Microsoft." *Fortune Magazine.* January 25, 2023.
https://archive.ph/rRvx1#selection-307.0-307.124

69. GotQuestions.org. "Home." *GotQuestions.org,* 3 Mar. 2008,
www.gotquestions.org/microevolution-macroevolution.html.

70. Berkley University of California. "What Is Microevolution? - Understanding Evolution." *Understanding Evolution - Your One-Stop Source for Information on Evolution,* 30 Sept. 2021,
evolution.berkeley.edu/evolution-at-different-scales-micro-to-macro/what-is-microevolution/.

71. "Human Genome Project Information archive1990–2003." *History of the Human Genome Project,* 7 June 2019,
web.ornl.gov/sci/techresources/Human_Genome/project/hgp.shtml
.

72. Truth Snitch. "Did the Human Genome Project Confirm Evolution?" *Truth Snitch,* 4 Aug. 2017,
truthsnitch.com/2017/03/08/human-genome-project-confirm-evolution/.

73. Kiprop, Joseph. "The Worst Floods in US History." *WorldAtlas,* WorldAtlas, 13 Oct. 2017, www.worldatlas.com/articles/the-worst-floods-in-us-history.html.

74. History.com Editors. "1900 Galveston Hurricane." *History.com,* A&E Television Networks, 9 Nov. 2009,

www.history.com/topics/natural-disasters-and-environment/1900-galveston-hurricane.

75. Betz, Bradford. "5 Of the Most Devastating Earthquakes in US History." *Fox News*, FOX News Network, 20 Feb. 2020, www.foxnews.com/us/5-of-the-most-devastating-earthquakes-in-us-history.

76. Rogers, Brooke. "Let me introduce you to George Washington Carver." Iowa State University Museums. 13 July 2020. https://www.museums.iastate.edu/virtual/blog/2020/07/13/let-me-introduce-you-to-george-washington-carver

77. Smith, Mariah, and Troy Lacey. "George Washington Carver: Journey from Slave to Scientist by God's Grace." *Answers in Genesis*, Answers In Genesis, 16 July 2021, answersingenesis.org/creation-scientists/george-washington-carver-slave-to-scientist/.

78. History.com Editors. "George Washington Carver." *History.com*, A&E Television Networks, 27 Oct. 2009, www.history.com/topics/black-history/george-washington-carver#:~:text=In%201921%2C%20Carver%20appeared%20before, which%20was%20seeking%20tariff%20protection.

79. Federer, William J. (2002). George Washington Carver: His life and Faith in His Own Words. St. Louis: Amerisearchm, p.36

80. "Simulating Physics with Computers http://www.cs.berkeley.edu/~christos/classics/Feynman.pdf", International Journal of Theoretical Physics, volume 21, 1982, p. 467-488, at p. 486 (final words)

81. McCracken, Harry. "IBM and MIT Kickstarted the Age of Quantum Computing in 1981 - Fast Company." *Fa0st Company*, 7 May 2021, www.fastcompany.com/90633843/1981-quantum-computing-conference-ibm-roadmap-mit.

82. Giles, Martin. "Explainer: What Is a Quantum Computer?" *MIT Technology Review*, MIT Technology Review, 20 Oct. 2021,

www.technologyreview.com/2019/01/29/66141/what-is-quantum-computing/.

83. Mann, Adam. "What Is Space-Time?" *LiveScience*, Purch, 20 May 2021, www.livescience.com/space-time.html.

84. Giles, Martin. "Explainer: What Is a Quantum Computer?" *MIT Technology Review*, MIT Technology Review, 20 Oct. 2021, www.technologyreview.com/2019/01/29/66141/what-is-quantum-computing/.

85. Giles, Martin. "Explainer: What Is a Quantum Computer?" *MIT Technology Review*, MIT Technology Review, 20 Oct. 2021, www.technologyreview.com/2019/01/29/66141/what-is-quantum-computing/.

86. Bucholz, Scott. Axelsen, Jacob Bock. Pham, Anh. Brown, Caroline. "Quantum Chemistry: Quantum Computing's Killer App Will Turbocharge R&D in Multiple Industries." Deloitte, 8 Nov. 2021. https://www2.deloitte.com/us/en/insights/topics/cyber-risk/application-of-quantum-computing.html.

87. Chen, Sophia. "Physicists, Lasers, and an Airplane: Taking Aim at Quantum Cryptography." *Wired*, 2 Feb 2017. https://www.wired.com/2017/02/physicists-test-quantum-cryptography-playing-catch-photons-plane/

88. Lardinois, Frederic. "IBM unveils its 433 qubit Osprey quantum computer." *TechCrunch*, 9 November 2022. https://techcrunch.com/2022/11/09/ibm-unveils-its-433-qubit-osprey-quantum-computer/.

89. Field, Hayden. "Meet the Man Building the Future of Quantum for IBM, Qubit by Qubit." *Emerging Tech Brew*, 9 May 2022, www.emergingtechbrew.com/stories/2022/05/09/meet-the-man-building-the-future-of-quantum-for-ibm-qubit-by-qubit?utm_campaign=etb&utm_medium=newsletter&utm_source=morning_brew&mid=42a6b4feb31ff661f3425339190ed0f9.

90. Shor, Peter. "This is No Clockwork Universe." https://math.mit.edu/~shor/No_Clockwork_Universe

91. Irving, Michael. *Information Teleported between Two Computer Chips for the First Time*, New Atlas, 27 Dec. 2019, newatlas.com/quantum-computing/quantum-teleportation-computer-chips/.

92. Smith, Sonia. "Celebrating the 50th Anniversary of JFK's Moon Speech." *Texas Monthly*. 21 Jan 2013, https://www.texasmonthly.com/the-culture/celebrating-the-50th-anniversary-of-jfks-moon-speech/

93. Warnke, Sue. "5 Steps to God: My Testimony." *5 Steps to God: My Testimony*, Leanership.org, 14 Sept. 2019, www.leanership.org/post/5-steps-to-finding-god.

94. Warnke, Sue. "5 Steps to God: My Testimony." *5 Steps to God: My Testimony*, Leanership.org, 14 Sept. 2019, www.leanership.org/post/5-steps-to-finding-god.

95. Companies Market Cap. "Companies Ranked by Market Cap." *CompaniesMarketCap.com - Companies Ranked by Market Capitalization*, 2022, companiesmarketcap.com/.

96. Google X. "Moonshot Mindsets." https://x.company/moonshot/

97. Google X. "Moonshot Mindsets." https://x.company/moonshot/

98. Metz, Cade. "Gary Starkweather, Inventor of the Laser Printer, Dies at 81." *Gary Starkweather, Inventor of the Laser Printer, Dies at 81*, The New York Times, 15 Jan. 2020, www.nytimes.com/2020/01/15/technology/gary-starkweather-dead.html.

99. Discovered, Just. "Invited Talk by Gary Starkweather, Laser Printer Inventor. Part 1." *YouTube*, YouTube, 5 Jan. 2017, www.youtube.com/watch?v=PiLDiWh6iBY.

100. Bingham, Nathan W. "A Christian in Silicon Valley: An Interview

with Gary Starkweather." *A Christian in Silicon Valley: An Interview with Gary Starkweather*, Ligonier Updates, 3 Feb. 2012, www.ligonier.org/posts/christian-silicon-valley-interview-gary-starkweather.

101. Metz, Cade. "Gary Starkweather, Inventor of the Laser Printer, Dies at 81." *Gary Starkweather, Inventor of the Laser Printer, Dies at 81*, The New York Times, 15 Jan. 2020, www.nytimes.com/2020/01/15/technology/gary-starkweather-dead.html.

102. Alcindor, Nicole. "YouVersion Bible app amasses over 500M installs on devices worldwide." The Christian Post, 12 Nov 2021. https://www.christianpost.com/news/youversion-bible-app-amasses-over-500m-installs.html.

103. Peters, Adele. "How to Unleash Creativity on the World's Biggest Problems, from ..." *How to Unleash Creativity on the World's Biggest Problems, from Alphabet's Moonshot Division*, 12 Feb. 2020, www.fastcompany.com/90462942/how-to-unleash-creativity-on-the-worlds-biggest-problems-from-alphabets-moonshot-division.

104. Vallotton, Kris. *Spiritual Intelligence: The Art of Thinking like God.* BAKER BOOK HOUSE, 2021.

105. Strathern, Paul. *Mendeleyev's Dream: The Quest for the Elements.* New York: St. Martin's Press, 2000.

106. Portocarrero, Edwina, David Cranor, and V. Michael Bove. "Pillow-Talk." Proceedings of the fifth international conference on Tangible, embedded, and embodied interaction (2011): n. pag. Web.

107. Turner, Rebecca. "10 Dreams That Changed Human History." *World of Lucid Dreaming*, 12 Mar. 2014, www.world-of-lucid-dreaming.com/10-dreams-that-changed-the-course-of-human-history.html.

Made in the USA
Las Vegas, NV
25 November 2024

12592158R00134